TEACHERS'
STRANGEST®
TALES

Other titles in the STRANGEST series

Cricket's Strangest Matches
Football's Strangest Matches
Golf's Strangest Rounds
Kent's Strangest Tales
Law's Strangest Cases
London's Strangest Tales
Medicine's Strangest Cases
Motor Racing's Strangest Races
Rugby's Strangest Matches
Running's Strangest Tales
Sailing's Strangest Tales
Shakespeare's Strangest Tales
Tennis's Strangest Matches

Titles coming soon

Cycling's Strangest Tales
Fishing's Strangest Tales
Horse Racing's Strangest Tales

TEACHERS' STRANGEST® TALES

Extraordinary but true tales from over
five centuries of teaching

IAIN SPRAGG

PORTICO

First published in the United Kingdom in 2016 by
Portico
1 Gower Street
London
WC1E 6HD

An imprint of Pavilion Books Company Ltd

ISBN 978-1-91023-298-9

A CIP catalogue record for this book is available from the British Library.

10 9 8 7 6 5 4 3 2 1

Reproduction by Colourdepth UK
Printed and bound by Bookwell, Finland

This book can be ordered direct from the publisher at www.pavilionbooks.com

CONTENTS

*Learning is never done without errors
and defeat.*

(Vladimir Lenin)

INTRODUCTION

Teachers' Strangest Tales is a celebratory, but above all comical, collection of the teaching profession's weirdest and most wonderful tales, as we delve into the educational annals to reveal how teaching has always been a calling that attracts a mixture of colourful characters, downright rogues and those who simply should never have been allowed through the school gates.

No one ever said it was easy being a teacher and in the pages that follow we shall explore just how testing life in and out of the classroom can really be.

From the more distant archives we'll learn all about the eighteenth-century Leicester swimming instructor who spent his spare time fighting bears, the hard-line headmaster who literally whipped a young Winston Churchill into shape and how Benito Mussolini, in his early incarnation as a schoolteacher, resorted to bribing his students with sweets.

From more recent times we will investigate the strange cases of the unfortunate teacher who was allergic to the classroom, and the hapless American educator who suffered from a morbid fear of children, as well as some of the most inappropriate and ill-advised ways devised by desperate teachers to keep their young charges in line.

From the UK there is the painful parable of the teacher who inadvertently shot one of his pupils with an air rifle, a deputy headmistress plagued by a flatulent chair and the Nottingham drama classroom that was suddenly transformed into the city's latest lap dancing venue.

Further afield we shall explore the incendiary story of the New Zealand teacher who burnt down his own school, the South African who recklessly bundled 19 kids into her Renault Clio, and the American art teacher who bunked off school to rob the local bank.

Education may be a serious business but – as *Teachers' Strangest Tales* proves – it also all too often makes a mockery of those who are either courageous or foolish enough to earn a living in the classroom environment.

Iain Spragg

THE FATHER OF FOOTBALL
LONDON, 1581

Sport can be a divisive subject in the staff room and often arouses passions that surpass even the altercations that all teachers have sadly witnessed over the years about missing cookies or flagrant misappropriation of the last of the milk. Sport is the subject on the curriculum that you either love or hate.

Athletic activities are vociferously championed by battalions of sports teachers up and down the country as absolutely vital for the increasingly sedentary Xbox generation and a great advert for healthy living and fitness. Their lessons, they argue, also teach pupils the essential life skill that is being able to jump over a triangular wooden box with a cushion perched on the top.

The naysayers, however, need no invitation to pour scorn on their colleagues, and maintain that prancing around the playing fields in a white T-shirt and trainers merely gets in the way of real education and proper subjects like maths and chemistry, and has absolutely nothing whatsoever to do with the fact they were always picked last for the hockey team when they themselves were at school.

One educator we can safely assume belonged firmly in the former camp was one Richard Mulcaster, the first headmaster of the Merchant Taylors' School in London and a man who definitely believed in the benefits of sport for his pupils. More specifically, Mulcaster was mad about football, and is widely credited with a lead role in the sixteenth century in transforming the sport from a lawless free-for-all into the more organised, beautiful game we recognise today.

'In England the game was still as rough and lacking in refinement as ever but it did at this time find a prominent supporter who commended it for other reasons,' reads Mulcaster's profile on the FIFA website. 'This supporter was Richard Mulcaster, the great pedagogue and head of the famous London schools of Merchant Taylors' and St Paul's. He pointed out that the game, if requiring a little refinement, had a positive educational value as it promoted health and strength. His belief was that it would benefit from introducing a limited number of participants per team and, more importantly, a stricter referee.'

Mulcaster set out his vision for football in his 1581 treatise entitled, deep breath now, *Positions Wherein Those Primitive Circumstances Be Examined, Which Are Necessarie for the Training up of Children, either for skill in theire Book or Health in their Bodie*, and he made it patently clear he believed the game needed to a bit more gentlemanly and less rowdy.

'Some smaller number with such overlooking, sorted into sides and standings, not meeting with their bodies so boisterously to trie their strength,' he wrote, 'nor shouldring or shuffing one another so barbarously ... may use footeball for as much good to the body, by the chiefe use of the legges.' He was also rather keen on players respecting the match officials.

'For if one stand by, which can judge of the play, and is judge over the parties, & hath authoritie to commande in the place, all those inconveniences have bene, I know, & wilbe I am sure very lightly redressed, nay they will never entermedle in the matter, neither shall there be complaint, where there is no cause.'

Footballers not arguing with the referee? Poor old Mulcaster will be turning in his grave.

SHAKESPEARE AT SCHOOL

LONDON, 1599

The staging of the school play can be a stressful time for those in the teaching profession. Ensuring a class of seven-year-olds are word perfect with their lines for the school's 'reimagining' of *The Cat in the Hat*, is a challenge on a par with teaching Barbary apes advanced rocket science, while the prospect of organising costumes for 20 Oompa-Loompas for the Year 6 production of *Charlie and the Chocolate Factory* has unhinged even the most hardened educator. Sourcing an acceptably docile donkey for the Nativity play is enough to give any teacher sleepless nights.

It is, though, not just amateur productions in junior academia that face challenges before the curtain goes up, and even the greatest dramatist the world has ever known once struggled to bring his work to the stage. We are of course talking about Mr William Shakespeare, the greatest exponent of the English language before the birth of Jeffrey Archer!

As every school child knows, the Bard wrote *Hamlet*. A searing examination of the human condition, it's generally acknowledged as one of his finest efforts and while we have no documented evidence for when *Hamlet* was first performed, clever scholars with beards and elbow patches believe the play most likely made its theatrical debut in 1599 in London.

Our Will was pretty content with the text for his seminal work but he wasn't initially happy with the action scenes. Specifically, he was worried about the swordplay that features heavily and, eager to attain a level of realism that would win over his fickle Elizabethan audience, he turned to the education profession for help. The man he turned to was an Italian teacher by the name of Salvator Fabris.

'Fabris was the fencing master of the King of Denmark and even, it would seem, of Shakespeare,' wrote Luigi Barbasetti in his book, *The Art of the Foil*. 'He is supposed to have suggested the technique of the assault which occurs in the fourth act of *Hamlet*.'

After receiving Shakespeare's immaculately penned SOS, Fabris caught the fastest boat available from Scandinavia to British shores to put Will's actors through their paces, and under his expert tutelage they quickly got to grips with the cut and thrust that was required. *Hamlet* duly premiered on the London stage and all those who saw the play remarked the sword scenes were the most realistic the English stage had ever seen.

Shakespeare's connection to teaching does not end there, however. We know surprisingly little about the Bard's life and in between 1585 and 1592 he fell off the documentary radar completely, academics dubbing the period his 'Lost Years'. A myriad of theories abound over what Will was up to while he was AWOL and many argue he earned a crust working as a schoolteacher before he found fame and fortune as a dramatist. One school of thought (sorry!) is that he worked for three years at Titchfield Grammar School in Hampshire.

'Because of his well-documented close relationship with the 3rd Earl of Southampton, we think it's a strong possibility he lived and taught here,' argued Kevin Fraser, the chairman of Titchfield Festival Theatre. 'It's such an interesting story. It's well known that William Shakespeare "disappeared" for a number of years and was a schoolmaster in the countryside. We should be on the Shakespeare map, there's no two ways about it.'

We can't be sure which subjects the Bard taught, if he did indeed work as a teacher in Titchfield or elsewhere, but it's probably safe to assume the world's greatest writer wasn't expected to take charge of sport or woodwork.

NEANDER'S NAME GAME
BREMEN, GERMANY, 1650

Teaching al fresco has always been a controversial topic in academia. Getting the kids out of a stuffy classroom and into the fresh air has obvious benefits, not least the opportunity it affords to top up one's tan, but trying to educate in the great outdoors does run the risk of falling foul of the elements and potentially hospitalising all those in the class suffering from acute hay fever.

A firm believer in getting out there was a teacher by the name of Joachim Neander, a chap who lived a short but remarkable life in seventeenth-century Germany and whose penchant for the outdoors saw him posthumously lend his name to one of the greatest scientific discoveries of the nineteenth century.

Born in Bremen in 1650, Joachim was the son of a Latin teacher and he followed his father into a career in education, becoming a private tutor in Heidelberg before, three years later, taking a job at a Latin school in Dusseldorf. Writing hymns though was his real passion and he penned 60 of them before his death; his 'Lobe den Herren, den mächtigen König der Ehren' ('Praise to the Lord, the Almighty, the King of Creation') is widely regarded as one of the greatest hymns in the Christian musical canon.

At the same time as he was penning his big religious hits while working as a teacher in Dusseldorf, Joachim liked to visit a nearby valley just outside the city and hold open air gatherings and deliver sermons to the locals. He died from tuberculosis at the age of 30 in 1680 (which may or may not have been linked to his readiness to embrace nature), but such was the impact of his al fresco gatherings that in the early nineteenth century the valley was renamed in his memory, becoming the Neandertal, *tal* being the German for valley.

So far, so good, but things got properly interesting a few decades later when miners unearthed some curious skeletons in a limestone quarry in the valley. The remains were identified by clever science types as prehistoric humanoids and duly dubbed 'Neanderthal Man'. Some 176 years after his death, Joachim had unwittingly christened the closest relatives on record to modern humans.

There was a distinct irony, however, in the decision to call the discovery Neanderthal Man. As a devout Christian, Joachim was presumably very much adherent to the 'God created mankind in his own image' school of thought, while the skeletons that took his name did rather back up Charles Darwin *et al* and the theory of natural evolution with little or no divine oversight.

What our dearly departed Joachim would have made of it all is a moot point. As a Latin teacher, skeletons weren't really his thing.

ALL HAIL HALE!

CONNECTICUT, USA, 1776

Teachers are not renowned as natural, reckless risk takers who readily embark on dangerous, extracurricular missions of derring-do. True, stepping into the classroom every morning is not without its dangers, not least that the little darlings might stop playing up long enough to listen and actually learn something, but on the whole the received wisdom is that educators tend not to be quite as adventurous as, say, Harrison Ford would have us believe with his portrayal of archaeology professor Indiana Jones in the eponymous film franchise.

There are, however, exceptions to every rule and the teacher with a wild side who concerns us here is called Nathan Hale. Our Nathan was a clever chap, a graduate with honours from Yale no less, and after his studies he decided education was his passion and in 1774 landed himself a job at the Union School in New London, Connecticut.

The history buffs among you will be well aware that the following year witnessed the start of the American War of Independence. Nathan was very much a patriot and in September 1776 he answered a call to join the New England Rangers, a quasi-military group set up by General George Washington with the remit of gathering intelligence. Or spying to you and me.

Washington, in particular, was desperate for information on the British plans to attack New York City and Hale was dispatched, disguised as a schoolmaster and carrying his Yale papers, to see what he could find out. Who was setting the homework and doing the marking while Nathan was gallivanting about behind enemy lines is a mystery.

Unfortunately for Nathan, before he had discovered anything worth reporting back to George, the Brits actually launched their attack and as he attempted to beat a hasty retreat to safety he was arrested by the Limeys. All sorts of incriminating documents were found on him – not least a two-week backlog of unmarked essays – and General Howe, the Commander-in-Chief of the British forces, ordered he be hanged as a spy. The next morning he was frog-marched to the gallows but before the rope went around his neck he famously told his executioners, 'I only regret that I have but one life to lose for my country.' His bravery in the face of death made him an American icon as the colonies struggled for freedom from Britain, and in 1985 he was officially designated the state hero of Connecticut. There are a myriad statues and memorials dedicated to him and schools named after him throughout the United States.

'He was an insignificant schoolteacher who never wrote anything important, never owned any property, never married or had children, never fought in a battle and who failed in his final mission but made history in the last few seconds of this life,' reads his profile on the *Early America* website. 'He is to be admired because of his courage in accepting a difficult mission (both dishonorable and dangerous) that he did not have to do. Then he had the cool and presence of mind to set the British straight about American patriotism, literally in the shadow of the gallows. Hale deserves to be remembered for his genuine dedication, his courage, and his willingness to pay the price with honor and dignity.'

LAMBERT'S LEICESTERSHIRE LIDO

LEICESTER, 1788

The expression 'larger than life' is one that frequently suffers from its overuse but in the case of famous, eighteenth-century Leicester resident and part-time swimming teacher Daniel Lambert, it could not be more aptly ascribed. Lambert was a very big fella indeed and when he was not instructing the youth of the city how to front crawl or back stroke, his appetite for both life, not to mention lunch, was legendary.

Born in Leicester in 1770, Lambert returned to the city as a teenager after an apprenticeship in Birmingham and succeeded his father as the keeper of the local gaol. When he wasn't banging up ne'er-do-wells, he was a renowned animal breeder and keen sportsman. Unfortunately he was equally renowned for his size, and by the age of 30 he was tipping the scales at an incredible 50st (700lb/318kg), making him, by contemporary accounts, the heaviest man on record in England.

But despite his waistline (and perhaps because of the extra buoyancy it afforded him) Lambert was a celebrated swimmer, and hordes of Leicester denizens would regularly approach him for swimming lessons. Lambert was happy to oblige and would take them down to the River Soar for tuition in the finer points of not drowning.

Legend has it that Lambert was such a powerful swimmer that he could plough his way across the river with two men lying on his back, but he was also apparently something of a no-nonsense, unsympathetic instructor (think Brian Glover's sports teacher character in *Kes*) and should any of his charges prove too timid or reluctant to dip their toes in the water, he'd leave their clothes on one bank of the Soar, carry them to the other and leave them to their own devices. He'd have definitely failed his school inspection had the inspectors come unexpectedly calling.

Lambert's fame, however, was not merely limited to his swimming exploits. On one occasion he was in the audience watching a dancing bear display in the city when the beast attacked his dog. After his pleas to its keeper to restrain the animal fell on deaf ears, Lambert proceeded to punch the bear to the ground and rescue his imperilled pet.

But back to the swimming lessons, which sadly did not make Lambert any real money and in his twilight years he was forced to relocate to London and charge people to visit him in his apartment, the prospect of a personal audience with the 50st man apparently enough to earn him a good living.

Lambert died in 1809 before he reached his fortieth birthday, but such is his legacy that in 2009 the *Leicester Mercury* newspaper described him as 'one of the city's most cherished icons'. Not bad for an erstwhile swimming teacher and part-time bear fighter.

THE SPECTRE OF THE SACK

LATVIA, 1845

The ability to be in two places at the same time would be a significant bonus for any overworked educator. The knack of preventing two pugnacious ten-year-olds from beating each other to a pulp in the playground, while simultaneously marking 5C's predictably dismal attempts at a literary critique of *Lord of the Flies*, would be manna from heaven and, let's face it, a great way of meeting whatever new Government targets had been introduced that particular week.

This strange tale, however, is an unsettling reminder that you should sometimes be careful what you wish for and concerns a young woman by the name of Emilie Sagée and her brief stint as a French teacher in the mid-nineteenth century. Our Emilie was educating the bright young things at the Pensionat von Neuwelcke, an exclusive girl's school in what is now modern Latvia. The 32-year-old was by all accounts diligent and well liked by her pupils but after a few weeks at the college the students' opinion began to change dramatically.

The problem was Emilie seemed to have a doppelganger. And the doppelganger was perversely fond of making its spectral appearances in the classroom just as the girls were trying to conjugate their verbs. On one occasion Emilie was writing on the blackboard when her ghostly double showed up, and although the phantom wasn't holding a piece of chalk, it proceeded to mimic her actions as she scrawled on the board. According to letters home by one of the girls, 13 students witnessed the scene. The doppelganger also turned up in the dining room one evening and silently mimicked Emilie as she ate, even though it was clutching neither knife nor fork.

Poor Emilie was reportedly oblivious to her uninvited double and, presumably in the interests of spooky variety, the doppelganger then took to materialising in one part of the school while Emilie was somewhere else altogether. It really freaked the kids out when it appeared in the teacher's chair in their classroom when all the girls could clearly see through the windows the 'real' Emilie gathering flowers in the school garden. Whether prompted by bravery or teenage stupidity, two girls actually approached the mysterious apparition and reported a strange resistance in the air when they reached out and tried to touch it. This was all witnessed by 42 pupils, so don't think the whole story is a fiction created by a bored schoolgirl with an overly vivid imagination.

Unfortunately for Emilie, rumours of her ghostly twin reached the parent body and the headmistress was rapidly bombarded with complaints that little Olivia was going to fail her French exams because of all the spooky shenanigans at the school, and Emilie was summarily sacked.

It later emerged that the doppelganger was not exactly a new phenomenon and Emilie had actually lost 18 teaching positions in the preceding 16 years thanks to her 'other half' and had 'accidentally' failed to mention she had a spectral double on her application form. The spontaneous hauntings abruptly stopped once Emilie had been dismissed and life at the Pensionat von Neuwelcke returned to its normal mix of forgotten homework, late-night feasts and implausible excuses for not doing cross-country runs.

HOME DISCOMFORTS
USA, 1850s

As many teachers will admit, if only in private, the best thing about the working day is home time. The departure of the hordes of little darlings back to the bosoms of their families, the descent of blissful peace and quiet and the opportunity to indulge in a hard-earned G&T, are all cause for celebration and further evidence of that old educational adage that teaching would be the best job in the world if it weren't for all the bloody kids.

Spare a thought, then, for the teachers in nineteenth-century America who dismissed their classes at the end of the day, packed their satchels and were then forced to endure the practice known as 'boarding round', a hateful tradition, which saw them lodging with the families of their pupils.

The poor teachers would spend an average of a week with one particular family before moving onto the next, and although their accommodation was free, most would probably have sold the family silver, had there been any, to avoid having to sleep under the same roof as a child they'd just spent six wasted hours trying to explain the mysteries of algebra to.

The standard of the accommodation wasn't always up to much either. 'I found it very unpleasant, especially during the winter and spring terms,' wrote one Wisconsin teacher in 1851. 'For one week I would board where I would have a comfortable room, the next week my room would be so open that the snow would blow in, and sometimes I would find it on my bed, and also in it. A part of the places where I boarded I had flannel sheets to sleep in; and the others cotton. But the most unpleasant part was being obliged to walk through the snow and water. I suffered much from colds and a cough.'

The bizarre and frankly awkward situation of a teacher sharing a house with a pupil (which would certainly invite the attentions of the local police these days) was further complicated by the fact that educators in the US of A back then were free to dish out all sorts of rather painful and, some would argue, sadistic punishments to students who displeased them. In some schools no one blinked an eye if a teacher thrashed a pupil with a ruler or stick, while in other schools it was deemed acceptable to force children to stand holding the heaviest book on the shelf out in front of them for an hour.

Good old-fashioned discipline, some might argue, but imagine the atmosphere over the dinner table *after* school as little Johnny, still smarting after receiving 20 of the best for failing to successfully name all the State capitals, sat down to break bread with a teacher who had just administered the punitive beating.

'Could you pass the salt please, Johnny?'

'No sir, I seem to be in rather a lot of pain, I'm badly bruised and I think my wrist is broken.'

TURNING IN TURNER'S GRAVE

BIRMINGHAM, 1877

Leaving an enduring legacy is something many teachers aspire to. Not quite as much as retiring at 55 with a full pension, the apartment in the Vendée paid for, obviously, and enough free biros to last a lifetime, but making a mark in the classroom that survives past lunchtime is definitely a good thing.

Inspiring a pupil to achieve greatness is one way to secure such a legacy as they wax lyrical in the future about your influence on them. Raising oodles of cash for charity never goes amiss if you want to be remembered fondly. Kidnapping the whole of the class will certainly ensure you're never forgotten, but we're looking for positive role models here, not the lead story on the evening news.

One teacher who definitely inspired generations of pupils was a nineteenth-century schoolmaster by the name of James Turner, who worked at King Edward's School in Birmingham. Unlike the vast majority of his educational peers, however, Turner did not have an Oxbridge degree and had, horror of horrors, never even been to university at all, but after he was given his first role at the school in the late 1850s, he was a stalwart of the staff at King Edward's for over 40 years, and legend has it never took a day off.

Quite a guy then and, according to local historians, such was his impact on the boys he educated that in 1877 one of them decided to pay tribute to their erstwhile schoolmaster by renaming Birmingham's Osborne Street, rechristening the road James Turner Street.

'The school had an important role in society at the time and the masters were very highly regarded,' explained King Edward's archivist Alison Wheatley. 'James Turner was not an ordinary teacher – he was not a graduate and he did not have a degree. He was just a talented boy who worked his way up through the ranks. At the time there were not many teachers who weren't Oxbridge classicists, so he was quite clearly highly thought of.

'Throughout his long career at King Edward's he would have taught many boys who went on to become the manufacturers, industrialists, town planners and developers of the city. So it is not beyond the realms of possibility that, as a highly regarded teacher, the street was named in his honour.'

An uplifting story perhaps, but the twist in the tale is the rather inconvenient fact that James Turner Street also happened to provide the setting for the UK Channel 4's controversial 2014 documentary *Benefits Street*, which depending on your perspective, was either a searing indictment of the struggles of society's disenfranchised or a shameless example of property porn commissioned with the sole purpose of making the middle classes feel superior.

In case you missed the original series, the amount of criminal activity on show – benefit fraud, shoplifting and cannabis cultivation – led to speculation over what the late James Turner would make of what had become of his urban legacy. We will never know, but it's probably safe to assume his famed work ethic would have put him on something of a collision course with the whole benefits culture the programme revealed, and he would not have approved of such fecklessness. Turner, of course, taught in an era when corporal punishment was permitted. Just saying.

WINSTON'S SCHOOL OF HARD KNOCKS

ASCOT, 1883

It's fair to say Winston Churchill was a resilient sort of chap. Masterminding Britain's defences against Germany during the Second World War certainly wasn't a job for the faint-hearted, and for a man who was partial to an ample supper, rationing was a bit of a pain as well.

Winston, of course, never flinched. He stood forever firm as London was subjected to the Blitz. He didn't blink as the Battle of Britain raged over the south of England. And he only permitted himself a few tears when Mrs Churchill insisted he cut down to 20 cigars and two bottles of brandy a day.

We can trace Churchill's remarkable fortitude back to his schooldays and his experiences at St George's School near Ascot which, according to the brochure, was a state-of-the-art educational facility but in reality was more akin to a house of pain. The future British Prime Minister arrived at St George's in 1883 at the age of eight and we can probably assume hated pretty much every minute of the experience.

'Undoubtedly [his parents] Randolph and Jennie had done some research and believed they had chosen a good school for Winston,' wrote Mary S. Lovel in *The Churchills: A Family at the Heart of History*. 'All the masters were highly qualified, it was bright and modern, had electric light (still considered a wonder and installed in very few homes, let alone in schools), a swimming pool and good sports grounds.

'What they could not have known was that the respectably married headmaster, the Rev. H.W. Sneyd-Kynnersley, was a sadist. According to the witness statement of a fellow pupil (forced by the demands of self-protection to assist the headmaster in these sessions by holding down the terrified victims), Kynnersley took positive pleasure in flogging small boys until they bled, or even excreted through fear and pain.

'This punishment was administered for the slightest indiscretion – for being late, or performing badly in an exam. Winston was renowned for unpunctuality and regularly had the lowest marks in his class throughout his school career …. He was one of those regularly singled out for corporal punishments.'

Winston himself would later remark that '[the floggings] exceeded in severity anything that would be tolerated in any of the reformatories under the Home Office', but he also once said 'famous men are usually the product of an unhappy childhood', and there was no doubt the brutal Rev. H.W. Sneyd-Kynnersely made him very unhappy indeed in his formative years.

In a perverse way, however, the nation owes a debt to the rabid Reverend for making Churchill the man he needed to become to save us from the evil machinations of Mr Hitler. But Winston would have his revenge on Sneyd-Kynnersely when he was elected Prime Minister, using his new powers to order an extraordinary rendition of the then 88-year-old former headmaster to a Japanese Prisoner of War camp. Which is absolutely not true at all.

CLASSROOM DICTATOR

ITALY, 1901

It is not uncommon for students to brand their teacher a fascist, particularly if they've just had the temerity to set their charges some homework, politely request that they stop playing games on phones they shouldn't have or, you know, actually try and educate them.

Benito Amilcare Andrea Mussolini was a proper, bona fide fascist, and before he got down to the serious business of ensuring the trains ran on time, executing his political opponents and condemning Italy to a humiliating defeat in the Second World War, 'Il Duce' enjoyed a rather colourful stint as a school teacher.

That Mussolini ever found work in a classroom is even more surprising considering he was twice expelled from school for stabbing fellow pupils. An excellent addition to the CV if your dream is to become a ruthless dictator perhaps, but hardly the type of behaviour cherished by the education system.

Nevertheless in 1901 Mussolini successfully completed his *diploma di maestro* and qualified as a teacher. He worked briefly in a secondary school before emigrating to Switzerland to avoid military service, but it's his second spell as an educator in 1906 after his return to Italy that concerns us.

His first job was at a school in Caneva, in the commune of Tolmezzo in the Venetian Alps, and suffice to say it was not a resounding success. Outside the classroom Mussolini began an affair with a local woman and contracted syphilis, and he fared little better at work, losing his job at the end of the year when police charged him with blasphemy and the school opted not to renew his contract. He managed to get himself another job at a private school in Oneglia, in northern Italy, but was subsequently sacked after launching a series of rhetorical attacks on the Catholic Church.

Mussolini's brief and chequered career as a teacher was at an end and by all accounts he was no great loss to the profession.

'All his biographers, and Mussolini himself, agree that he was not a good teacher,' wrote Peter Neville in his book *Mussolini*. 'The children (40 of them in the class) liked him, but he could not control them. He swore at them but they were not afraid of him, and he was reduced to giving them sweets to keep them in order.

'This makes the nickname the children gave Mussolini, *il tiranno* (the tyrant), somewhat ironic. Neither did his personal appearance do him any favours. He was often dirty with unlaced shoes and long, straggling hair (the famous bald pate came later).'

It was 18 years later that *il tiranno* became *Il Duce* when Benito rebranded, favouring new methods of murder, torture and intimidation to facilitate his ruthless rise up the political ranks, rather than relying on his old technique of dishing out free confectionary.

THE HEN-MAN'S REVENGE
NEW HAMPSHIRE, USA, 1906

Robert Frost was one of the most popular and critically acclaimed American poets of the twentieth century. It says so on Wikipedia, so it must be true. Frost also won four separate Pulitzer Prizes and was an exceedingly accomplished wordsmith who – and we're resorting to Wikipedia here again – was famed for his 'realistic depictions of rural life and his command of American colloquial speech, his work frequently employed settings from rural life in New England in the early twentieth century, using them to examine complex social and philosophical themes.'

A poetical heavyweight then, but before his verse began to pay the bills, Frost worked on a farm in New Hampshire which his grandfather had bought for him, amongst other agricultural pursuits raising White Wyandottes chickens in an effort, in his own words, to 'try to stop thinking'.

Sadly Frost proved ill-equipped for the farmer's life and in 1906 he turned to higher education to earn a crust, landing himself a job as an English teacher at a place called Pinkerton Academy in Derry, New Hampshire. He would spend five years at Pinkerton before his literary career really took off in the 1910s with the publication of his first successful poetry collection, *North of Boston*, but while he was generally regarded as a competent teacher, Frost didn't exactly display the patience or sense of humour most educators rely on to get through the day.

There was one incident in particular, referencing his days on the farm, which underlined his tetchy nature. 'One of Frost's students wrote "hen-man" on the blackboard in his classroom,' wrote David Sanders in his book *A Divided Poet*. 'Clearly feeling the epitaph as an insult, Frost was outraged enough to track down the culprit and insist on his expulsion, and though many, including the principal, urged leniency, the trustees backed Frost and the boy went.'

For a man with such a love of words, Frost showed himself to be surprisingly averse to avian allusions. Some argue his reaction was due to a genuine chicken phobia, which seems unlikely since he was the one who chose to raise the birds on the farm, while others have it was simply because Frost felt any nod to his time tilling the soil somewhat undermined his scholarly status at the school.

The upshot was our graffitist got his marching orders, but there is a degree of irony to the story because it was a certain Robert Lee Frost who once said, 'education is the ability to listen to almost anything without losing your temper or your self-confidence'.

Bobby lose his temper? Perish the thought.

A GANGSTER'S EDUCATION
CHICAGO, USA, 1913

Crime doesn't pay. It's true that in the past it has been known to fund the elicit purchase of extravagant yachts, opulent holiday homes and the services of any number of the finest plastic surgeons on the planet, but the salient point here is that the benefits of crime are fleeting (unless, arguably, you happen to be a trader in the City or on Wall Street or an insurance salesman) and sooner or later the long arm of the law will catch up with you. Society will demand the retribution and punishment will be meted out.

It happens to even the biggest fish in the criminal pond and they didn't come much bigger than Al Capone in his heyday. Mr Capone (as it was prudent to call him) was the boss of the 'Chicago Outfit', the gang from, well, Chicago which grew fat from the bootlegging business during the Prohibition Era. If you wanted a surreptitious drinkie in America in the 1920s, the chances were it was Capone's brew you were imbibing.

Capone enjoyed seven years at the top before Kevin Costner managed to get him jailed for tax evasion. Or was that in *The Untouchables*? Anyway, the point is that Capone's reign was brought to an abrupt halt when he was sentenced to 11 years in federal prison, and another criminal kingpin had bitten the dust.

So what on Earth has this got to do with teaching? Did Al go to some special school for crooks where he honed his gangster skills? Did he have a tutor two nights a week who taught him how to use a shot gun? Did he take a correspondence course in racketeering?

No, in fact young Al was a good student growing up in Brooklyn. The education system was tough – as the son of immigrants he was subject to prejudice and the occasional beating – but Capone stuck to his studies diligently. A change of school, however, and the onset of his teenage years dramatically changed all that.

'The new school, called Public School 133, was a hideous Gothic monstrosity, as impersonal and forbidding as its name, a massive building that bore more resemblance to a prison than a place of learning,' wrote Laurence Bergreen in *Capone: The Man and the Era*. 'There he consistently received Bs on his report card, until the sixth grade, when his grades began to disintegrate. He was often truant, missing school more than half the time, and his absences took their toll on his studies.

'By the time he was ready to go on to the seventh grade, Al Capone was 14 years old. That year his adolescent frustration and impatience with school finally exploded. After being scolded by his teacher one time too often, Al lashed out at her. She struck him and he hit back. Since hitting was common in these schools, the incident might have ended there, but then the teacher took him to the principal, who administered a sound beating to Al. Afterward, the boy vowed never to return to P.S. 133, and he never did.'

What he did do was join the Brooklyn Rippers and then the Five Points Gang and he had essentially swapped a traditional education for a hands-on apprenticeship in crime. It evidently stood him in good stead, rising as he did to become 'Public Enemy Number One' according to the newspapers, and one of the most notorious gangsters of the twentieth century.

It would be harsh to suggest his teacher and his headmaster were *responsible* for Capone's subsequent life of crime but they probably did have some unintentional part to play in him going spectacularly off the rails. It certainly made for a very anxious retirement for them both when they realised their former pupil had grown up to become the country's most feared Mafia boss.

MURDER ON THE BERLIN TO PARIS EXPRESS

GERMANY, 1914

They say the first casualty of war is innocence, but in the case of the First World War, it would be more accurate to say the first casualty of the conflict was actually an unfortunate schoolteacher by the name of Henry Hadley.

For years the history books related the conventional wisdom that Private John Parr was the first fatality of the conflict, shot in action in Belgium in late August 1914 just three weeks after Britain had declared war on Germany, but recent research has revealed it was in fact Hadley who was the first to shuffle off this mortal coil a mere three hours after the fateful declaration of hostilities.

Poor Henry was 51 years old in 1914. Public-school educated, he became a languages teacher and just happened to be working in Berlin as Europe found itself on the verge of bloody conflict. When Germany declared war on France on 3 August, Henry knew Britain would inevitably be drawn into the imminent dust-up and jumped onto a train bound for Paris, from where he planned to depart for England.

En route to France, however, he had a row with a waiter in the buffet car and then became involved in a 'heated exchange' with a group of German officers. He returned to his seat, but his fatal mistake was to get up and resume his argument with the soldiers, one of whom suddenly drew a revolver and shot him in the stomach at point blank range. 'They have shot me, Mrs Pratley,' he said to his housekeeper and travelling companion. 'I am a done man.'

Poor old Henners however didn't die there and then. He was rushed to hospital and clung on for another 24 hours but by three o'clock in the morning of 5 August he had breathed his last. The British Prime Minister, Herbert Asquith, had declared war on the Germans at midnight.

'He was the first British casualty of the Great War and the first person to die as the direct result of enemy action,' said military historian Richard van Emden, who unearthed Hadley's sad tale after reading Mrs Pratley's account of his untimely demise.

'Henry Hadley just happened to be in the wrong place at the wrong time. He also seems to have made the mistake of upsetting an armed German officer in the atmosphere of heightened tension as the whole of Europe plummeted into war. Having spent two decades researching and writing about the Great War, his story is, to me, an amazing, fresh discovery.'

When news of Mr Hadley's death reached London, the Government demanded an explanation from Germany but they wouldn't play ball and 'rebutted all claims of foul play.' The German officer who shot him, Lieutenant Nicolay, insisted he had only opened fire because Mr Hadley was 'acting suspiciously', was 'vague about his travel arrangements', and had raised a stick at him when confronted. He was, of course, only following orders.

Poor Mrs Pratley didn't come out of the incident unscathed, either, whisked off as she was to a German military prison for interrogation. She was suspected of being a spy but persuaded her captors she was simply a housekeeper by rustling up a sensational shepherd's pie.

FICTION FRICTION

ETON, 1917

The whole student-becoming-the-master theme is a common one in literature and film. When, for example, Darth Vader renews acquaintances with Obi-Wan Kenobi in *Star Wars* he says that 'When I left you, I was but the learner, now I am the master', and then rather graphically underlines the point by slicing his former teacher in half with his lightsaber.

All good teachers, of course, want their pupils to blossom, although not necessarily into homicidal maniacs, with a distinctly S&M taste in fashion. A prosperous, successful pupil reflects well on the efforts of the educator but there are limits and teachers who are overshadowed by their charges can sometimes get frightfully indignant indeed.

Our eclipsed educator in this case is none other than Aldous Huxley, the acclaimed writer and poet, and erstwhile teacher. Huxley is most renowned for his seminal work *Brave New World*, published in 1932, and at the time generally acknowledged as the go-to tome for a visceral imagining of a Dystopian future.

That is until 1949, when George Orwell's *Nineteen Eighty-Four* was published and rather stole Huxley's thunder when it came to a dark vision of a future dominated by omniscient Government, loss of personal freedom and misery unbounded. Everyone acknowledged *Brave New World* was still jolly good, you understand, but *Nineteen Eighty-Four* was really rather special.

That alone must have galled Huxley, but to add insult to injury, it transpired that Orwell was a former pupil, Huxley having taught him French for one year at Eton. The pupil had well and truly become the literary master.

Orwell had not forgotten Huxley and sent him a preview copy of *Nineteen Eighty-Four.* Huxley replied with a thank-you note and while his letter is initially upbeat, describing the book as 'profoundly important', it is not long before he succumbs to the temptation to be critical.

'The philosophy of the ruling minority in *Nineteen Eighty-Four* is a sadism,' he wrote, 'which has been carried to its logical conclusion by going beyond sex and denying it ... Whether in actual fact the policy of the boot-on-the-face can go on indefinitely seems doubtful. My own belief is that the ruling oligarchy will find less arduous and wasteful ways of governing and of satisfying its lust for power, and these ways will resemble those which I described in *Brave New World.'*

So basically he's arguing he's right and Orwell has got it all wrong, that the means of oppression employed by the Establishment in *Nineteen Eighty-Four* are pie in the sky. Huxley does stop short of ordering Orwell into detention but he's evidently not happy that his former pupil's effort has outshone his own.

Which, presumably, is exactly how those who taught the likes of Leonardo da Vinci, Albert Einstein or Stephen Hawking felt when they first handed in their homework.

HIGHER PAY
FOR THE HIRSUTE
ARKANSAS, USA, 1920s

By any measure of normality you wish to employ, some folk from the American state of Arkansas are distinctly odd. Endearingly eccentric if we're being polite here; stark raving mad if we are not.

Its state capital Little Rock has, after all, been the venue for the World Cheese Dip Championship every year since 2010, while the city of Stuttgart has been hosting the annual World Championship Duck Calling Contest, 'the largest-ever organized recognition of aptitude in the field of fowl mimicry', for nearly 80 years.

Since the 1940s, residents of Arkansas have been convinced a 7ft (2.1m) hairy interloper with piercing red eyes dubbed 'the Fouke Monster', aka Bigfoot's cousin, has been roaming the land and, before it closed down, tourists could wile away a few bizarre hours at 'Digpatch USA', a theme park based on cartoon hillbillies.

Arkansas – crazy name, crazy place. Unsurprisingly the state also boasts some 'unusual' laws that make for interesting reading. It is, for example, illegal for men to ask women to dance during the month of July. In the town of Fayetteville, dogs are not permitted to bark after 6p.m. and it is apparently illegal to buy or sell blue light bulbs in the state. In Little Rock, it is a legislative no-no to eat cheese on Friday, unless you order a large bottle of beer to wash it down with while, for reasons that remain intriguingly unclear, new parents are forbidden to christen a child Zabradacka.

Another bizarre edict that dates back to the 1920s – and here, patient reader, is where we finally return to the matter in hand – stated that female teachers who had their hair cut in a short, bob style could not legally be given a pay rise. That's right, if you were educating the children of Arkansas, you happened to be of the feminine persuasion and you liked your hair manageable, you couldn't earn a few extra dollars.

The logic behind this surreal financial prejudice against the less hirsute has sadly been lost in the midst of time and we can only speculate why those with a fuller head of hair were deemed worthy of potentially greater remuneration. Maybe they believed the bob was a bit, you know, militant? Perhaps they were worried that what might be deemed a less-than-ladylike look would corrupt Arkansas young girls. Or was it that the authorities secretly owned shares in L'Oréal and were worried that too many shorthaired educators would hit profits?

Mercifully female teachers in the state can have whatever style they choose these days, although it is still frowned upon, albeit privately, if they opt for a crew cut back and sides with a bright pink perm atop. That goes down like a lead balloon in the annual pay review.

THE PSYCHOTIC PHILOSOPHER

AUSTRIA, 1926

There is, we are frequently informed, a fine line between madness and genius. It's a maxim that is as relevant to the world of education as it is wider society, and for every inspirational teacher, think Robin Williams in *Dead Poet's Society*, there is a sadistic nutjob, very much akin to Miss Trunchbull in Roald Dahl's *Matilda*.

The distinctly schizophrenic teacher who concerns us here goes by the name of Ludwig Josef Johann Wittgenstein. An acclaimed Anglo-Austrian philosopher, Ludwig was a very clever chap indeed and his 1921 book, *Tractatus Logico-Philosophicus*, is considered a modern classic, if you like that sort of thing. Ludwig worked at the University of Cambridge for nearly 20 years, and such was his fierce intellect his one-time teacher Bertrand Russell (who was no thickie himself) described his former pupil as, 'the most perfect example I have ever known of genius as traditionally conceived; passionate, profound, intense, and dominating.'

Quite a boffin then, but Ludwig was a troubled soul, and three years after writing *Tractatus Logico-Philosophicus* he suddenly decided to turn his back on academia, give away the family fortune and become a primary school teacher in rural Austria. He ended up in a tiny village called Trattenbach and set about educating the local kids.

At first, at least, his stint in the sticks was a successful one as he introduced a wide-ranging new curriculum to his pupils. 'They designed steam engines and buildings together, and built models of them,' wrote Spencer Robins in *The Paris Review*. 'They dissected animals; examined things with a microscope Wittgenstein brought from Vienna; read literature; learned constellations lying under the night sky; and took trips to Vienna, where they stayed at a school run by his sister Hermine.'

Ludwig, however, was not happy. 'I am still at Trattenbach,' he wrote in a letter to Russell, 'surrounded, as ever, by odiousness and baseness. I know that human beings on the average are not worth much anywhere, but here they are much more good-for-nothing and irresponsible than elsewhere.'

In 1924 he left Trattenbach and joined a nearby school in Otterthal, but it was here that his teaching career really went off the rails as his undisputed genius took a back seat, and madness took a firm hold. In April 1926 during a lesson, he became so infuriated by an 11-year-old pupil called Josef Haidbauer, that he hit the boy over the head three times. Haidbauer collapsed unconscious and Ludwig was in seriously hot water. 'I called him all the names under the sun,' raged one parent after hearing what had happened. 'I told him he wasn't a teacher, he was an animal trainer! And that I was going to fetch the police right away.'

He didn't hang around to face the music, however, beating a hasty retreat back to Vienna. The incident was reported to the police and a court case ensued but, after undergoing a psychiatric report, Ludwig was exonerated. The rumours at the time were his influential family had pulled strings to make the whole beastly business go away. Remarkably he was able to get a job teaching philosophy at Cambridge just three years after hospitalising one of his pupils.

He returned to Austria a decade later to ask for forgiveness from Haidbauer and the other pupils he had manhandled, but apparently got something of a lukewarm reception from the good folk of Trattenbach and Otterthal. Ludwig, of course, had hoped they would all be 'philosophical' about it.

AUDEN'S AL FRESCO INSPIRATION

HEREFORDSHIRE, 1933

All of us at some point during our long days at school have come across a 'maverick teacher' – the eccentric educator with flagrant disregard for the rules and figures of authority and whose only goal is to unlock the hidden talents of all those they instruct by whatever crazy and unconventional means necessary.

Every school has one. They tend to be young, idealistic English or perhaps history teachers, rather than Mr Griffiths and his metalwork class, but the salient point is that education is always awash with individuals who like to stir things up a bit.

The acclaimed Anglo-American poet W.H. Auden was one such classroom maverick. Like many writers before and since, Wystan (for that is what the 'W' stands for) worked as a teacher both in the UK and in the US of A before his embryonic literary career really took off and he was, by all accounts, a rather 'interesting' character.

'Auden was a moralist who drank too much, a homosexual who thought homosexuality wicked, a subversive who chose to write in pedantically traditional verse forms, an eccentric opposed to the romantic theory of personality, a man obsessively punctual, sartorially sloppy,' read a profile in *The New York Times* in 1981. 'As a personality, Auden is a type of manic schoolmaster. He taught at British boys' schools and the University of Michigan and the New School for Social Research and Swarthmore, always conveying the impression that he was brilliantly deranged, with his bitten fingernails and nonstop smoking. [The poet] Louis MacNeice said of him, "Everything he touches turns to cigarettes". From one classroom to another he carried with him the tone of the math mnemonic he'd had to memorize as a child: Minus times Minus equals Plus.'

One of his first teaching jobs was at the Downs School in the Malvern Hills in the early 1930s, and it was here in leafy Herefordshire that Auden took his eccentricity to new heights, dragging his bed out onto the school lawns and sleeping under the stars during the summer months. Quite what the children made of seeing their teacher grabbing 40 winks outside the headmaster's office is debatable but, like any poet worth his salt, Auden did not let the unconventional experience go to waste and in 1933 he penned 'A Summer Night', a poem all about his al fresco repose. The first paragraph went like this ...

Out on the lawn I lie in bed
Vega conspicuous overhead
In the windless nights of June,
As congregated leaves complete
Their day's activity; my feet
Point to the rising moon.

Literary critics generally agree 'A Summer Night' is one of Auden's finest poems, and far superior in both its imagery and impact to others he wrote while teaching at Downs, variously entitled 'Out of Red Biro Again', 'Lumpy Custard for Lunch' and the frankly woeful 'School Inspection Tomorrow'.

THE PLAINFIELD PRESS PRANK

NEW JERSEY, USA, 1941

Depending on your point of view, university education departments are either venerable bastions of academic excellence, where the educators of tomorrow studiously learn their trade or, as some maintain, centres of riotous, hedonistic excess where graduates spend two years drinking their own body weight in snakebite before having to go out into the real world and actually, you know, teach some kids.

The lines between studying to teach and actually teaching became bizarrely blurred back in the 1940s, however, when Plainfield Teachers College in New Jersey hit the back pages in the USA, making rather a sporting name for itself courtesy of the exploits of the school's all-conquering American football team.

Plainfield's finest, it seemed, were far from borderline alcoholics, they were actually fine athletes. The college's football team was sweeping all before it and every week *The New York Times* and *The Philadelphia Record* carried the side's scores and reports of Plainfield's magnificent players. The star of the show was sophomore running back Johnny Chung, aka the 'The Celestial Comet', who was noted for eating bowls of steamed rice between quarters to keep his energy levels high, while the Plainfield team was expertly guided by an innovative coach by the name of Hop-Along Hobelitz.

If you're not beginning to get a whiff of a rodent, you should be because it later transpired that Plainfield, its unbeaten team, Johnny, Hop-Along *et al* were completely fictitious.

'It all started when an avid sports fan named Morris Newburger and a couple of friends got together one Saturday after the stock market closed and had some drinks,' explained *The Westfield Leader*, a local New Jersey newspaper. 'Newburger had become a fan of Slippery Rock Teachers College, whose score always appeared in the Sunday list of college football scores. On the spur of the moment, he decided to call *The New York Times* and said "I want to report a score, Plainfield Teachers 21 (his secretary was from Plainfield) Regency 12."

'The next morning, there was the score in *The New York Times*. Newburger and a friend decided that they would call every week, Newburger to the New York papers, his friend to the Philadelphia papers. They often forgot to make sure they had the same opponent and the same score, but whatever.'

The hoax continued for six admittedly humorous weeks. No one apparently noticed that Plainfield's scores in *The New York Times* were different to those published in the *Philadelphia Record* but the team's results did generate a buzz, and the prank finally unravelled when a reporter called Red Smith from the aforementioned *Record* decided to take a trip to New Jersey to see what all the fuss was about.

When Red arrived in Plainfield he could find not a trace of the football team. More pertinently, he couldn't find a teacher training college either and the game was up, so to speak. Newburger wrote one final press release under his *nom de plume* 'Jerry Corden' explaining that the team had been forced to cancel its remaining fixtures because Chung and his team-mates had failed their exams and the Plainfield Teachers College American football team was no more.

A fictitious school where students play a complicated and ridiculously violent sport? If only J.K. Rowling had thought of that …

REWRITING THE HISTORY OF E-READERS

SPAIN, 1949

Read, read, read. And then read some more. It's the mantra of all self-respecting educators and the espousing of books as the font of all knowledge is paragraph one, page one of *The Beginner's Guide to Good Teaching*. Reading, in short, represents the path to educational enlightenment and a wheelbarrow full of good erxam results.

The advent of the Kindle (other electronic reading devices are available) has rather revolutionised the whole world of books. *The Complete Works of Shakespeare*, for example, was once an invaluable but undeniably cumbersome tome, but today it is but one per cent of the memory of your lightweight and eminently portable Kindle. Your average eReader doesn't even blink when you download *War And Peace* and *Sons and Lovers* at the same time, while J.K. Rowling's entire oeuvre doesn't even make a dent in the storage capacity of a Kobo Aura. The point is you can store a hell of a lot of books, educational or otherwise, on a modern, electronic thingy.

But before the Kindle was even a glint in Amazon's eye, there was the 'Mechanical Encyclopedia', an ingenious invention by a Spanish schoolteacher by the name of Angela Ruiz Robles, back in 1949. To describe her device as ahead of its time would be an understatement.

Angela was concerned with the weight of books her pupils

were forced carry in their school bags. A kindly soul, she wanted to make reading more accessible and practical, and after hours at the drawing board she came up with the Mechanical Encyclopedia, a machine which worked with pressurised air, allowing users to add different spools to the device containing text content. It was, in short, an eReader without any electronics.

'It has some coils where you place the books that you want to learn in whatever language,' read the covering note she sent with her patent application. 'By a movement of the same [the coils] it passes over all the topics, making it stop where you would like it to.'

Ingenious indeed, but sadly Angela was met with a deathly silence when she went in search of funding for her invention, even when she outlined her ambitious plans to add a zoom function, reading light and calculator to the device. 'There were other priorities in the country and they went for other projects,' María José Rodríguez Fortiz, a professor at the University of Granada, told Spanish media.

'In her later years Angela tried to resurrect the project, when everything was technologically viable. But she did not manage to secure public or private funding.'

Angela's working prototype is now on display in the National Museum of Science and Technology in La Coruña, a testament to the vision of a humble Spanish schoolteacher who didn't want her beloved pupils straining their backs carrying their copies of *Don Quixote* to class. Amazon should really be paying Angela royalties but since she passed away in 1975, and given the company's 'dubious' record on meeting its corporate tax obligations, don't hold your breath.

WALT'S EDUCATIONAL LEGACY

PENNSYLVANIA, USA, 1954

The Disneyfication of the world is a phenomenon long documented and ever since Disney released *Snow White and the Seven Dwarfs* back in 1937, the company has cut something of a cultural swathe across the world with its animated offerings. In 2013 alone the behemoth created by Walt Disney had an estimated net worth and market capitalisation of $103.96 billion. Not bad for a company whose primary attraction is cartoon animals and a few rollercoasters.

Teachers, of course, are acutely aware of the power of Disney. Since 2013 and the release of the all-conquering *Frozen*, it's nigh impossible to enter a classroom and not risk injury tripping over a *Frozen* ruck sack, a *Frozen* pencil case, *Frozen* lunch box or even (and this really is available) a *Frozen* toilet seat. Merchandise inspired by *Toy Story*, *Cars* or *Wreck-It Ralph* is equally ubiquitous. Almost.

It's irksome indeed, but spare a thought for the poor teachers over in Pennsylvania who spend their working day educating America's finest at the Walt Disney Elementary School, an entire building dedicated to celebrating everything about the world's biggest purveyor of cinematic cartoons.

The Walt Disney Elementary School was born in 1954 when the local education authority was in the process of building a new school in the town of Levittown. Some bright spark decided to canvas the kids what they thought should be the name of the new school but rather than follow the traditional route of going for the name of a historical figure like George Washington, they all screamed they wanted to be educated at Walt Disney Elementary.

To be fair, it's hard to blame the kids. The market was flooded at the time with Disney books, Disney magazines and Disney toys. Cinemas were dominated with Disney productions while The Mickey Mouse Club and Disney TV shows led the TV ratings. Sound familiar?

The school asked Walt Disney himself if he would attend the official opening ceremony. Smelling some good publicity, he agreed and also despatched a series of artists to decorate the new building with a series of wooden character murals, as well as art and animation cells to festoon the walls. In short, he Disneyfied the hell out of the place.

And so, even 60 years later, the pupils and teachers alike are confronted with a constant barrage of Disney images. The door to each class is labelled the 'Mickey Room' or 'Donald Room', the principal's office is entered past a 'Captain Hook' sign while the girls and boys toilets are known as 'Mermaid Lagoon' and 'Pirates Cove' respectively. You get the full, horrendous picture. The rate of sick leave taken by teachers at the school is three times the national average. Possibly.

Walt Disney popped his clogs in 1966, and while the empire he founded continues as a licence to print money and our school in Pennsylvania still proudly bears his name, Walt's personal legacy appears somewhat diminished. 'It's sad that many of the children who today attend the school,' admitted principal Fay Manicke in 2010, 'look up at the large framed photograph of Disney in the school lobby and ask, "Who's that?"'

The clue's in the name kids, it's in the name.

THE MISCHIEVOUS BEATLE

LIVERPOOL, 1955

Many teachers have presided, albeit unwittingly at the time, over the education of pupils who subsequently go on to find fame, fortune or even infamy in later life. It's extremely hard to believe that George W. Bush or David Beckham spent much time in the classroom before leaving their dubious imprint on the public consciousness, but the point is famous people go to school just like the rest of us mere mortals.

Back in 1955 the teachers at Quarry Bank High School in Liverpool had a teenager by the name of John Winston Lennon under their educational wing. You may be aware that John went on to enjoy limited success in the music industry with a popular beat combo called *The Beatles* but, of course, his teachers were unaware what the future held for little John. What they did know was that he was a right pain in the neck.

According to school records John's misdemeanours were myriad, and between May 1955 and February the following year, the man who would go on to write *Come Together*, *I am the Walrus* and *Strawberry Fields Forever* was put in detention a grand total of 29 times.

His litany of crimes included making 'foolish remarks', 'not wearing school cap' and 'impertinence'. He was also guilty of 'fighting in the classroom', being a 'nuisance' and showing 'no interest whatsoever'. On two separate occasions he managed to earn himself three detentions in a single school day and he really pushed the rebellious boat out when he failed 'to report for class detention'. The little scamp.

His teachers at Quarry Bank must have been pulling their hair out, but according to one of his educators at least, his CV of indiscipline was not the full story. 'The sheet is typical of John Lennon, he was an extremely cheeky boy', said Peter Beech, his general science teacher. 'He did, however, know his limits. In the classroom, if you settled John down, you generally settled the class down. His chemistry teacher said that John could actually go far'.

It's doubtful that said chemistry teacher envisaged his pupil becoming a global pop star – he probably foresaw a bright future for Lennon as a Bunsen burner salesman – but it was certainly a prescient observation.

Details of John's chequered educational career came to light when Quarry Bank had a bit of clear-out, and just as his school report was about to be consigned to a bonfire, someone noticed his name on the paperwork and saved it from the flames. In 2015 it was put up for auction in a Sotheby's Rock and Pop sale and fetched a princely £2,500. 'There is no denying that we are still living in a capitalist world', Lennon said in an interview with *Playboy*, of all titles, in 1981 and a price tag of £2,500 for his old school report card rather emphasises his point.

THE RANNOCH REPTILE WRANGLER

PERTH AND KINROSS, 1959

A headmaster needs to be a no-nonsense figure, very much the enforcer of any educational establishment, the go-to man for colleagues if pupils get a little unruly or rebellious. And while the prospect of being sent to see the headmaster is a threat to be used sparingly, it's been known to reduce even the most recalcitrant student to subservience in a matter of seconds.

The halcyon days of the disciplinarian head honcho have now gone forever, but if there was ever a headmaster you didn't want to mess with it was Dougal Greig, the erstwhile leader of the Rannoch School in Scotland and a man so tough he made Rambo look like a wimp.

Dougal helped establish Rannoch, on the shores of the loch of the same name in Perth and Kinross, in 1959. Before that he had served with the Air Sea Rescue service during the Second World War, fearlessly pulling downed pilots out of the North Sea and later from the Atlantic Ocean off the coast of Sierra Leone.

Legend has it that while headmaster at Rannoch he lost his finger while trying to fix a malfunctioning fire alarm and proceeded to drive himself to hospital in the school ambulance, his severed digit tucked away in a matchbox, just in time to get it successfully reattached by surgeons.

However, it is his exploits during the war that really cemented his reputation as a seriously tough cookie. 'While stationed in Freetown he braved shark-infested waters to free his propeller and went nocturnal crocodile hunting on the Sierra Leone River, which served as a runway for Sunderland flying boats patrolling the Atlantic,' read his obituary in *The Scotsman* following his death in 2013.

'It was full of crocs, a dangerous hazard to locals, and armed with a rifle and searchlight he and his colleague would hunt them down from their launches. On one memorable occasion, with their quarry wounded but still alive, Greig leapt overboard, landing up to his knees in mud, and threw a rope round the astonished croc's jaws before both he and it were dragged back to the boat. In due course, some of the crocodile's hide made its way back to Edinburgh in the shape of a handbag for his mother.'

The ability to wrestle a crocodile would, of course, make the prospect of getting even the most intransigent teenager to fall into line a walk in the park, and while Dougal was thought of fondly by his charges at Rannoch, let's just say maintaining discipline was not an issue.

His time at Rannoch was brought to a somewhat premature end by illness and the school finally closed down in 2002 but not before its remarkable headmaster had provided his pupils with some indelible memories. 'During his time in charge he made sure the school was not just a place of learning, it was also part of the community. It helped with mountain rescue operations and had its own ambulance and a lifeboat, serving Loch Rannoch,' ran his obituary in *The Herald*. 'The lifeboat, however, was not entirely successful. Purchased second-hand in Edinburgh, its engine and hull were carefully restored at the school. However, at its official launch ceremony – and with Mr Greig at the helm – it gracefully entered the water and promptly sank. The former coxswain had to be rescued by the Loch Patrol.'

THE ILLITERATE EDUCATOR

USA, 1961

There are number of qualities it is generally agreed are jolly handy to possess if you want to cut it in the teaching game. Not having a silly, possibly rude, surname is very high indeed on the list for would-be educators, closely followed by a wardrobe completely bereft of anything made from corduroy, and the ability to endure the agony of a six-week summer holiday.

There are, of course, the more prosaic qualities required, such as the patience of Job, the love of imparting knowledge to a new generation and a certain flourish with a red biro.

The absolute numero uno requirement, however, is the ability to read and write. Schools are really rather strict about this stipulation whenever they advertise a job, and illiterate teachers are about as numerous as North Koreans who are able to enjoy a luxury overseas holiday.

Amazingly however, from time to time educators who can neither read nor write do get jobs in schools. One such man was John Corcoran and for nearly two decades he worked as a teacher in America with the authorities, his colleagues and his students none the wiser that the written word was all something of a mystery to him.

John started to struggle academically at an early age but (and don't tell the kids this!) cheating can get you a long way and he graduated High School despite his illiteracy. He nailed a place on an athletic scholarship at the University of

Texas in El Paso thanks to his sporting prowess and some brazen lying and, even more remarkably, he emerged in 1961 with a bachelor's degree in Education and Business Administration.

One of the first jobs he was offered out of college was as a High School social studies teacher. John took it and for the next 17 years he managed to pull the wool over everyone's eyes.

'It was wrong of me to have been in the classroom without the necessary skills,' he said after coming clean in the early 1990s. 'Many of my students said I was their favourite teacher or a "good teacher", but I don't want just good teachers in the classroom. I want excellent, superior teachers in the classroom. As a teacher, it really made me sick to think that I was a teacher who couldn't read. It is embarrassing for me, and it's embarrassing for this nation.

'Life is full of mysteries. Why I became a teacher after graduating from college and reading only at a second grade level will have to remain one of those life mysteries. There was a series of circumstances leading up to this decision, some of which included my need for a job after graduation and being offered three different teaching jobs because there was a shortage of teachers. I had no plans after college and in my wildest dreams I never thought that I'd be a teacher.

'There wasn't the written word in there [in my lessons]. I always had two or three teacher's assistants in each class to do board work or read the bulletin. The students wrote their names on a seating chart and then pronounced them for me. To avoid reading the list, I asked them the next day to call out their names, claiming I wanted them to get to know one another.

'I can remember when I was eight years old saying my prayers at night saying, "Please, God, tomorrow when it's my turn to read please let me read." You just pretend that you are invisible and when the teacher says, "Johnnie, read", you just wait the teacher out because you know the teacher has to go away at some point.

'It was much more of a moral dilemma being the teacher who couldn't read than the boy, teenager or even college student who couldn't read. I have apologized publicly for my crimes, sins, and trespasses for the adult decision I made. Sharing my story also invites literates to consider the horrendous impact of not teaching little boys and little girls how to read.'

To his credit, John has since learned to read and write, become a literacy campaigner and in 1994 published his book *The Teacher Who Couldn't Read*. It's not the greatest title the literary world has ever come up with but John's a brave fella for holding his hand up to his subterfuge, so we can let that pass for now.

ED GOES AWOL

MAINE, USA, 1963

The pressures of the goldfish bowl existence that is life in the classroom is enough to make any teacher temporarily snap. The daily stress of facing 30 or more little faces at such close proximity can send even the most mentally resilient educator around the bend, and which teacher hasn't at least once looked at themselves in the mirror after a tough day at the office and wondered whether they weren't going, you know, a little bit bonkers.

A particularly arduous day of educating certainly seemed to do for a 40-year-old fifth grade teacher by the name of Edward Spearin over in the USA in 1963. Poor Ed knocked off as usual one day and headed home to his apartment but was rather understandably befuddled and bemused when he woke up, nearly a fortnight later, in his car parked up in a layby. He had absolutely no memory of how he got there and, to further compound the mystery, he was a full 350 miles (563km) from home. 'I had two or three days growth of beard,' Ed said later, 'and I couldn't recall how I got there and where I was.'

He decided the only course of action was to pay a visit to the local police station to see if the boys in blue could be of assistance. He urged them to call the Superintendent of Schools in his hometown of Waterville and said superintendent, Mr Burford Grant, confirmed Ed had been reported missing after failing to show up for work.

'A Maine teacher awoke yesterday morning in Meriden and realised he had been an amnesia victim – that he could not recall where he had been and what he had done the last 13 days,' reported the local newspaper. 'Dr Albert DiGiandomenico, police surgeon, after examining Spearin, stated the teacher may have had a seizure of amnesia. He advised Spearin to seek medical attention on his return to Maine. Detective Caffrey said Spearin appeared well mannered and well kept, but was bewildered on appearing at the station. An oddity was noticed by police. There were three bunches of raw carrots and three packages of peanut crackers in the automobile. Spearin, a United States Army veteran of the Italian campaign in World War II with service from 1942 through 1945, is a graduate of Washington State Teachers College.'

A seizure of amnesia? It certainly sounds serious and while the medics were never able to definitively identify the cause of Ed's sudden memory loss, suspicious glances were inevitably cast in the direction of Waterville's most challenging fifth grade students. The raw carrots and peanut crackers were a little bizarre but surely it would have been stranger had the police officers discovered *cooked* carrots on the back seat of his motor.

KISS IN THE CLASSROOM
NEW YORK, USA, 1970

The injudicious application of make-up is a common cause of conflict between teachers and pupils. Weary school staff are forever ordering rebellious students to remove excess eyeliner and expunge illegal lipstick, and while rules is rules and teachers definitely hold the moral high ground, they invariably have to ruin it by adding 'It's not Paris Fashion Week, you know' to the end of every exchange.

Even discreet make-up is discouraged in the school environment but what is absolutely a complete no-no is an industrial plastering on of the products, a really heavy-duty dosage of the Max Factor or Maybelline. And definitely not a loving homage to the Gene Simmons look, the front man of the popular heavy metal combo *Kiss*, and a man famed for cementing his face with white foundation before applying a liberal amount of black make-up around his eyes to create his iconic 'demon mask'.

Whether Mr Simmons was wont to turn up in class wearing aforementioned stage make-up during his brief stint as a teacher in New York is an intriguing thought. Gene's sojourn as an educator lasted only six months, instructing sixth graders in Spanish Harlem, but if he brought even an ounce of his flamboyant stage persona to his lessons they must have been an entertaining, albeit slightly disconcerting, blast.

Simmons graduated from Richmond College in 1970 with

a degree in education and could speak four languages – English, German, Hungarian and Hebrew – and before he found fame belting out such hits as 'I Was Made For Lovin' You' and 'Rock and Roll All Nite', he landed a job at Public School 75 in New York City.

His lessons were unconventional to say the least and he incurred the wrath of the principal when he replaced a Shakespeare play with a Spiderman comic book on his students' curriculum.

He soon realised, however, that a life in the classroom was not for him and handed in his notice, although his reasons for quitting are unclear. 'I used to be a sixth-grade teacher in Spanish Harlem,' he said in one interview. 'I did it for six months and I wanted to kill every single kid.'

That, Gene thought, might make him sound a little 'murdery' and in a subsequent chinwag with the press, he offered an alternative explanation. 'The reason I quit is that I discovered the real reason I became a teacher. It was because I wanted to get up on stage and have people notice me. I had to quit because the stage was too small. Forty people wasn't enough, I needed 40,000. For the short time that I taught sixth grade I've often wondered if I would have been any good. Really good, you know, not just a teacher who gets by and collects his $500 a week. Would I have made a lasting impact on those pupils?'

You would if you had worn the make-up, Gene, just maybe not in the way you hoped.

NESSIE'S WATERY GRAVE
SCOTLAND, 1972

April Fools' Day is a date dreaded by some in the teaching profession, giving as it does their already unruly charges an annual, legitimised excuse for japes, high jinks and further general disruption. Teaching the little darlings can be hard enough without the pupils trying to knock off school early, claiming they've got to get to Buckingham Palace to receive an MBE from the Queen for services to education.

Some teachers, however, embrace the annual opportunity for a spot of tomfoolery, and this strange and rather sophisticated tale illustrates perfectly that, contrary to popular opinion, there are some in the business with a sense of humour.

Our mischievous educator goes by the name of John Shields. Back in the early 1970s John was the resident education officer at the Flamingo Park Zoo in Yorkshire, and in 1972 he and some colleagues headed north to Scotland for a bit of a field trip. More specifically, they travelled to the Highlands and Loch Ness on a mission to prove that the eponymous local monster existed. Apparently the team had developed a new 'hormone sex bait' that Nessie would find irresistible and lure the beast from the depths, where presumably John or one of his chums would be poised with a camera.

On the morning of the last day of March, the group were tucking into a hearty breakfast at their hotel when the manager burst in breathlessly and informed them a strange object had been spotted in the loch. It was all hands to the boat and 20 minutes later the intrepid team returned dragging what appeared to be Nessie's dead body behind them. Eyewitness reports said the corpse was between 12 and 18ft (3.6–5.5m) in length and weighed one-and-a-half tons. 'I touched it and put my hand in its mouth,' said one stunned local. 'It's real, all right. I thought it looked half-bear and half-seal, green in colour with a horrific head like a bear with flat ears. I was shocked.'

The discovery was worldwide news and the next morning, 1 April obviously, newspapers across the planet reported the sad news that the Loch Ness Monster was now definitely extinct. The Highlands Tourist Board went into meltdown.

The team were going to haul Nessie south of the border for further inspection, but the Fifeshire County police department had other ideas and impounded the huge cadaver and asked Michael Rushton, general curator of the Edinburgh Zoo, to come and give the discovery the once-over. He prodded and probed expertly and quickly declared the carcass before him was not Nessie but in fact an elephant bull seal. The cheers from the Highlands Tourist Board could be heard for miles.

'It is a typical member of its species,' Rushton told the media. 'It's about three to four years old. I have never known them to come near Great Britain. Their natural habitat is the South Atlantic, the Falkland Islands or South Georgia. I don't know how long it's been kept in a deep freeze but this has obviously been done by some human hand.'

That human hand was, of course, our John, who quickly confessed to the prank. The seal, he admitted, had been brought to the UK from the Falkland Islands by a team of scientists. It had lived briefly at Dudley Zoo in the West Midlands but was acquired by John after it had died. He had then shaved its whiskers off, padded its cheeks with stones and popped it in the deep freeze for a week before surreptitiously transporting it to Loch Ness. John himself had phoned the hotel manager with the anonymous tip-off.

As April Fools' Day jokes go, it was certainly elaborate, while the image of John shaving the corpse of an elephant seal is nothing if not disturbing. John at least got a lot of laughs for his efforts but went too far the following year when he impaled a defenceless donkey with a javelin and claimed he discovered a unicorn.

EDUCATIONAL IRE IN ISLINGTON

LONDON, 1979

We don't need no education,

We don't need no thought control,
No dark sarcasm in the classroom,

Teachers leave them kids alone,
Hey teacher leave them kids alone,

All in all it's just another brick in the wall,
All in all you're just another brick in the wall.

The immortal lyrics to Pink Floyd's seminal 1979 hit 'Another Brick In The Wall (Part II)' and a song for all the anti-educationalists (is that a real word?) out there if ever there was one. Stick that in your satchel and polish it, Department for so-called Education.

The song, of course, famously features the haunting vocals of a group of schoolchildren to give the track that authentic feel, and the story of how 23 pupils from Islington Green Comprehensive in north London came to collaborate with the greatest ever exponents of Prog Rock is, as you can imagine, an interesting one. If you're sitting comfortably, then we shall begin.

The resident music teacher at Islington Green was an unconventional chap by the name of Alun Renshaw, a chain-smoking, skinny jean-wearing maverick by all accounts, who fought the law even though the law won. Sorry wrong iconic British band there.

One day Pink Floyd's manager and sound recordist were dispatched by Roger Waters to locate some young vocal talent for the track and they ended up at Islington Green, around the corner as it was from the recording studio. Crucially they bypassed the headmistress's office *en route* to Alun's class and asked whether he could supply any singers. Alun said they'd come to the right place and after a few rehearsals marched 23 of his class to the recording studio. Crucially he also bypassed the headmistress's office as they made their way out.

The song was recorded and the Floyd had a gigantic, worldwide hit on their hands. The only problem was Islington Green's headmistress, Margaret Maden, and the local education bigwigs were not best pleased, what with the kids singing a song that wasn't exactly flattering about the whole school experience and all. The Inner London Education Authority called the whole sorry episode 'scandalous', while Margaret got it in the neck for giving permission for the kids to leave school, her cries that she'd done no such thing falling on deaf ears.

'I viewed it as an interesting sociological thing and also a wonderful opportunity for the kids to work in a live recording studio,' Alun said some years after the event. 'We had a week where we practised around the piano at school, then we recorded it at the studios. I sort of mentioned it to the headteacher, but didn't give her a piece of paper with the lyrics on it. When I saw what the lyrics were, of course, I went "Oops". I had to go and talk to Margaret about it. By that time, of course, it was a bit too late to back down.'

Surprisingly, Alun wasn't sacked for his part in the incident, but he did beat a rather far-flung retreat not long after 'Another Brick In The Wall (Part II)' was released, emigrating to Australia. It left Margaret to face the music, so to speak, but she insists she holds no grudges towards her erstwhile colleague.

'I'd rather the horrors of the Pink Floyd episode hadn't happened,' she admitted. 'But if I had to choose that happening as opposed to Alun Renshaw, I'd choose Alun being there any time, any day because he had a good effect on the children. He made a difference to their lives. I think schools, and I think children, need that kind of eccentric nutter, as long as they're producing the goods. A school couldn't have nothing but Aluns, it would collapse instantly.'

It's the 23 kids who lent their voices to the song who we should really be feeling sorry for, however. The hit made Pink Floyd squillions but all the children got was a lousy copy of the single and the album and tickets to a concert. To avoid further bad publicity they weren't allowed to appear on *Top of the Pops,* and because they didn't have Equity cards, they weren't even allowed to 'play themselves' in the video. In 2004 the 23 launched a legal action to claim back unpaid royalties for their seminal performance on the track, but at the time of going to press the courts had sadly still not reached a decision on whether Islington Green's finest warblers would get a penny for their melodic efforts.

VLAD'S VOCAL PREPARATIONS

LONDON, 1990

There's an old saying that you can choose your friends but you can't choose your family. It's not strictly true these days if you're, say, adopting a child from China or undergoing designer IVF treatment, but the point largely stands and is one which all those unfortunate enough to be related to Kim Jong-un, the head of the Ku Klux Klan, or indeed Simon Cowell, sincerely wish wasn't the case

It's also an adage which could seamlessly be applied to the sphere of education. Teachers can pick their school, perhaps even select their class but they've got no choice when it comes to the students. You get what you're given.

Kevin Scanlan learned this educational truism in 1990 when he was working as a private English tutor in London. Our Kev was doing all right for himself, instructing rich foreign types in the finer points of the language of Shakespeare and Wordsworth, but one day was booked to give a one-on-one lesson to a Russian gentleman on Oxford Street, accompanied by a burly 'companion', that left him retrospectively rather shaken.

'When I walked in, he shook my hand and asked if I would like a glass of white wine. There was an unopened bottle in an ice bucket. In the end neither of us had any. I thought it was a bit strange as it was only nine in the morning. He was polite and pleasant enough, but I got the strong impression that, if pushed, he could be dangerous. His face was cold and detached.' Kev did his thing and left but years later he was watching the TV and saw the face of his former pupil looking back at him. Kev had unwittingly been teaching Vladimir Putin how to speak better English.

It transpired that back in 1990 a 38-year-old Vlad had just finished a four-year stint in Germany working for military intelligence, and before heading home to Mother Russia to work for the KGB he was ordered over to Britain to brush up on his Ps and Qs, presumably in preparation for telling a succession of British Prime Ministers in their native tongue that he'd fly his planes in whoever's airspace he damn well pleased.

'The other thing that struck me was how short he was,' added Kev unwisely whilst having lunch in a London sushi bar after learning the identity of his mystery student. Rumours that the first English phrase Putin demanded to be taught was 'What is the quickest route to Crimea?' is scurrilous hearsay. And risks a visit from some burly chaps with easy access to small amounts of nuclear materials.

SIGUROUR'S SUGGESTIVE COLLECTION

ICELAND, 1997

The nirvana of retirement is something many weary teachers yearn for. After all those years in the front line of the battle to educate future generations, a bit of time off is the least they deserve, and at the time of going to press, retired teachers had not yet had their hard-earned pensions purloined by the Government.

However, like any soon-to-be OAP, former educators must face up to the dilemma of what to actually do with all their extra free time. There are sadly only a finite number of quiz shows with which to while away the hours, while Samba for Beginners at the Town Hall only accounts for Tuesday nights. Regardless of size, alphabetising the CD collection is a day's worth, maximum.

After 37 years in the educational ranks in his native Iceland, it was just such a quandary that confronted Sigurour Hjartarson when he finally turned his back on the classroom in 1997. The now ex-history and Spanish teacher at Hamrahlid College in Reykjavik had time on his hands, but what do with it?

Sigurour immediately ruled out joining the bowls club and instead decided to open a museum, and so the Icelandic Phallological Museum was born. Yes, that is right, Sigurour founded a museum dedicated solely to celebrating penises. Willies. Or, if you wish to be more scientific about it, the male reproductive organ.

An unconventional idea, granted, but as Sigurour explained, his fascination with male members had been kindled as a child when he owned a bull's penis (or 'pizzle'), which had been given to him to use as a riding crop. He quickly earned a reputation as the 'willy man', friends began to bring him whale penises from nearby whaling stations and his collection began to grow.

By 2006, the museum boasted some 245 specimens (pickled in formaldehyde or dried out) on display from a wide range of native Icelandic species, and some penile exhibits from further afield, including a 3¼ft (1m) long elephant appendage. The biggest preserved John Thomas from the animal kingdom on display was a 5½ft (1.7m), 154lb (70kg) whopper from a sperm whale, while the smallest was a hamster penis, which stretched to a modest eight-hundredths of an inch (2mm) in length and had to be viewed through a magnifying glass.

'Somebody had to do this', explained Sigurour. 'It was just a hobby, they were not on display in the sitting room. I hope visitors leave the museum in a better mood than when they arrived. It's mainly Americans who are squeamish about this. Maybe at first people were astonished and thought that I was queer or something was wrong with me but on the whole, it has been pretty successful and the reaction has been good.'

The museum moved premises in 2004 when it relocated from Reykjavik to the fishing village of Husavik, 300 miles (483km) north-east of the capital, but it was in 2011 that the bizarre collection really hit the headlines, when Sigurour acquired the one specimen he had always wanted.

If you're squeamish, it's probably prudent to skip the next few paragraphs because, yes, we really are talking about Sig adding a man's penis to his museum shelves. An actual penis from a *Homo sapiens*.

The member in question was donated to the museum by a 90-something Icelander by the name of Pall Arason.

Something of a local celebrity and renowned womaniser who liked to brag about his 'outstanding sexual performances', Arason wanted his gentleman's sausage preserved for prosperity. In 2011 he stopped getting jiggy with it on a permanent basis and Sigurour had the missing piece of his genital jigsaw.

Unfortunately the embalming of Arason's pride and joy wasn't quite as successful as was hoped, and although it is on display at the museum, Sigurdur is considering donating his own manhood to the collection when he cashes in his chips.

'His organ had shrunk quite a bit,' he said. 'Unfortunately the process of preservation wasn't successful at all. The problem is, I'm getting old and I'm shrinking like Mr Arason. So I'm not sure that my son [who took over as curator of the museum in 2009] would like me when the time comes.'

So not quite as large an, ahem, endowment as 'Mr Lover Man' Arason had originally hoped to bestow, then.

DRESSED TO IMPRESS

STAFFORDSHIRE, 1997

The iconic mortarboard is as synonymous with education as riotous assemblies and geography homework. Let's overlook for now the fundamental design flaw, which imperils the eyes of unsuspecting pupils should the wearer bend down and blind a student with one of the headwear's four lethal corners, the mortarboard is a timeless symbol of academia.

They are, of course, a rarer sight in classrooms today than they were a century ago. Times change and sadly the mortarboard is no longer *de rigueur* with teachers who wish not to become a laughing stock in front of their charges, but there are educators still bravely trying to preserve the tradition.

One such man was supply teacher David Austin, who was working at Torc High School in Staffordshire in the late 1990s. The headmaster at the school was, it seems, also a devotee of the mortarboard and accompanying gown ensemble and David decided to copy the example set by his boss and don the full scholastic regalia. The outfit, he reasoned, lent the wearer a certain air of scholastic authority.

Unfortunately David's attempts to look authoritative apparently failed and he claimed he was sacked as a direct result of sporting the iconic hat and cloak combo. 'It was just a simple case of follow my leader and it worked,' he said. 'The kids couldn't think of an argument against it.

It might seem bizarre but all I was doing was following my boss. There are a huge number of people in offices all wearing black suits – their bosses wear black suits.'

Staffordshire County Council refused to confirm David's assertion that he was handed his notice as a direct result of his sartorial choices. 'We can confirm he was employed by the school,' a spokesman said, 'and he left in 1997.' The mystery of why David really lost his job has never been definitively resolved.

His departure from Torc was not, however, the only time that David was in the news, and in 2012 he was making headlines again when he was hauled in front of the General Teaching Council accused of unacceptable conduct. One school alleged his teaching style was too 'abrupt and demanding', while the headmistress at another college maintained he had accused her of lying in front of one of the students.

His appearance at the GTC hearing was nothing if not bizarre. He turned up wearing his mortarboard and gown, which was probably not a smart move given what he claimed had transpired at Torc, and for the first 90 minutes of proceedings he refused to speak, claiming his regional accent would prejudice his case. He communicated instead by writing on an overhead projector.

His unusual behaviour perhaps predictably failed to impress the panel sitting in judgement over him and they banned David from the classroom for two years. 'I retain a passion appropriate to teaching,' he said after the verdict, 'and sadly that appears not to be respected by this arm of the profession.'

Whether David has now hung up his mortarboard and gown for good is unknown. His adherence to the 'old skool' look is commendable, but there's a counterargument that just as corporal punishment in schools has had its day, it might now be time to consign the mortarboard to the dustbin of sartorial history.

THE COST OF A GOOD EDUCATION

GEORGIA, USA, 1999

Every teacher has encountered pupils they just cannot abide. As model professionals they wouldn't admit it in public, of course, but all educators have their private *bêtes noires*, the disruptive students who they'd happily shove off the edge of a cliff if they thought they could get away with it. Savannah Technical College maths teacher Theodore Brown had two such pupils. They were ladies by the name of Amanda Glover and Rechon Ross, and to say his two educational charges got up Brown's nose would be an understatement. He really couldn't stand the pair.

Brown accused Glover of refusing to buy a textbook required to take his course and of disrupting his lessons by borrowing books from other students. He also claimed she verbally abused him on at least three separate occasions and embarrassed him in front of the rest of the students, causing him mental and emotional distress.

He accused Ross of defamation and embarrassment and also alleged she caused problems for him with his supervisors and damaged his career prospects and emotional well-being.

It was quite the list of grievances and Savannah being in the state of Georgia in the USA – and our American cousins famously being rather fond of litigation – Brown decided to sue Glover and Ross for the damage he alleged they had caused to his professional reputation. A reasonable man, he decided to demand the tiny, merely symbolic sum of $100 million in punitive damages from his erstwhile pupils.

The school refused to comment on the whole horrid business of one of their teachers taking two of its students to court but the girls refused to be intimidated and countered with the rather pithy response that the only thing they were guilty of was trying to get an education. Even by American standards, it was a surreal lawsuit and most saw the funny side. 'Even the sheriff's deputy who served me with the paperwork was laughing,' Ross told reporters.

Brown, however, was most definitely not laughing. He refused to elaborate on the exact nature of the 'blemishes' on his career record he alleged had been caused, but defended his right to go to court, and dismissed suggestions that even if he won the case, Glover and Ross were highly unlikely to have $100 million between them down the back of the sofa. 'This is America,' he said. 'You heard about the man that only had $23 in his bank account the morning he hit the lottery for $187 million. You never know what people have.'

Sadly not even the allegedly omniscient World Wide Web can shed any light on the outcome of Mr Brown's litigious riposte to his pupils' alleged misbehaviour. There is no record of the case actually making it to trial and maybe common sense prevailed (although this is still America and the law we're talking about here) and the courts told Brown to sling his hook and get a life.

The moral of the story, however, is never, ever upset anyone in the States. There are packs of ravenous lawyers lurking behind every corner – and they bite.

A WHITE HOUSE HOAX

BUCKINGHAMSHIRE, 2000

Unattended students are, most teachers would ruefully concede, an unfortunate incident just waiting to happen. The unaccustomed freedom afforded by the conspicuous absence of an adult educator is too much for most youngsters, and many stressed teachers who've briefly vacated the classroom in search of their daily Valium have returned only to be confronted by scenes of havoc it took the combined talents of the Visigoths, Vandals and Huns years to wreak on mainland Europe.

Pupils left to their own devices just cannot be trusted, but a quartet of ten- and 11-year-old boys at Thorpe House School in Buckinghamshire took the 'while the cat's away the mice will play' theme to a whole new level in 2000 just before their Christmas holidays, when they decamped to the computer room sans supervision, fired off a few emails and subsequently found themselves the subject of a major, transatlantic FBI investigation.

The lads weren't looking for trouble, but with not even a supply teacher in sight, they went online and happened upon the official website of the home of the President of the United States, the White House. The site invited users to email Mr President, who at the time was Bill Clinton, and the young chaps sent a couple of innocuous messages wishing the Commander in Chief and his missus Hilary, a Happy Christmas. Festive goodwill, however, quickly turned to mischief and the third email was rather incendiary, reading as it did, 'Send me $1 million or I will blow up the White House'. Half an hour passed uneventfully but with no cash windfall forthcoming, the lads followed up with another ill-advised missive. 'I still have not received my million dollars,' one typed. 'It is now $2 million or I will blow up Texas'.

They thought nothing more of it until they returned to school after Christmas and were hauled into the headmaster's office, who informed them he had just got off the phone with Special Branch, who had had an interesting conversation with the FBI, who had been talking to the Secret Service, and what the hell did they think they were playing at threatening to vaporise the most powerful man in the free world.

'It was a bolt from the blue,' admitted Thorpe House's head. 'It's not every day you get a call from Special Branch. I wasn't sure at first that it wasn't a friend having a joke.' The Special Branch officer said it was a serious matter and they had to investigate it because he had to report to the Americans that it had been dealt with.

'He took the view that it was best for the school to deal with the boys as it saw fit and he said he would tell the Americans that there was no serious threat. They never thought in a million years that somebody would take it seriously. They realised the full gravity of it once it was explained to them. The boys were very ashamed and they were even more sheepish when their parents found out.'

The boys were mortified, but did point out that if the Americans really thought they were terrorists with explosive capabilities, why had they received automated replies from the White House website 'thanking them for their interest'. What they didn't realise was that Bill was too busy to reply personally, otherwise occupied as he was in the Oval Office with a private 'meeting' with one of his interns.

KNITWEAR TO THE RESCUE

ITALY AND KENT, 2001

The school trip is always a nervous time for teachers. The responsibility of looking after other people's kids is onerous enough when they're confined to scholastic barracks and you can send them home after six-and-a-half hours but heading out into open country for days on end is taking *in loco parentis* to extremes. It's little wonder, then, that the first item to go in most teachers' hand luggage before embarking on the dreaded school trip is a family-sized bottle of vodka.

It was with understandable trepidation that the teachers of Rainham School for Girls in Kent agreed to take a group of Sixth Formers skiing in Italy. The prospect of corralling a bunch of teenage girls was daunting enough, but with the inherent dangers associated with winter sports, it was a trip laden with potential pitfalls.

Remarkably the trip passed uneventfully until the final day of fun and frivolity in the Dolomites, when 16-year-old Holly Ashdown was skiing down a beginner's slope, lost control on an icy bend and fell over. Sadly her classmates failed to capture the moment for posterity (or even Facebook), but Holly's indignity quickly turned to danger as she tumbled 60ft (18.3m) down a slippery slope (are there any other kind?) and alarmingly found herself heading for the edge of a cliff. It was her lucky day, however, as her left ski snagged in a small tree – but her right leg was hanging over the edge of the precipice and there wasn't a single St Bernard in sight.

Step forward maths teacher, Ian Mitchell, who quickly calculated the distance between Holly and safety (finally proving his oft-repeated assertion to his students that trigonometry is useful in real life) and launched a heroic rescue bid that would have made any survival expert proud.

'I knew I had to get below Holly and make her safe,' Ian said. 'I asked for the other children's scarves and tied them in a reef knot so I could get myself down to her. When I reached her I tied the scarves around a tree and then around Holly. I looked at the flimsy twig she was snagged on and knew I had to do something else because the scarves weren't strong enough to hold her. The fact there was also a vertical drop next to her scared me.'

The air ambulance was called and although it took two hours for the mountaineers to climb up the cliff and get to Holly, she was safely bundled off to hospital on a stretcher, the worst of her injuries some minor bruising.

'I went into a spin and fell over,' she said after her ordeal. 'The next thing I remember was sliding down the slope feet first on my stomach. I was screaming and yelling. When I came to a stop my right leg was dangling over the edge of the cliff. I definitely think someone was looking out for me and watching over me.'

Yes Holly, his name was Ian. The party from Rainham School duly returned home from their eventful school trip the following day, where Ian received a hero's welcome, the like of which no maths teacher had ever experienced before or since. His act of derring-do, however, proved to be a one-off as the following year's trip erred on the side of caution, and sent the Sixth Form to the nearby and altogether less perilous Lillyputt Mini Golf centre in Broadstairs.

AN UNFRIENDLY WEBSITE
LINCOLN, 2002

Remember Friends Reunited? It was the *de rigueur* social media website of the Noughties before the brazen *enfants terribles* that are Facebook and Twitter came along, but for a while Friends Reunited was top dog, and all those who yearned to learn what happened to their first crush from primary school, or the bully who put custard down their pants, were drawn like helpless moths to the website's irresistible flame.

Friends Reunited was responsible for many things. Obviously it reunited old friends – doing exactly what it said on the tin – but its not-so-secret remit was to afford people the opportunity to gauge whether they were doing better in life than their erstwhile classmates. It was also responsible for rekindling many romances that had begun years ago behind the bike sheds, and such was the amount of hanky-panky going on, one leading divorce lawyer warned: 'If you value your marriage, do not visit this site'.

Our Friends Reunited tale unsurprisingly concerns a teacher and a historic legal case in 2002 which, with the benefit of hindsight, would open the floodgates for the legal profession to grow exceedingly fat on the proceeds of social media litigation.

Our inadvertently pioneering educator was Jim Murray, who was happily enjoying his well-earned retirement after more than three decades of service in the classroom, when he happened upon Friends Reunited and a post by a former pupil, one Jonathan Spencer. If Jim was hoping Jonathan had gone online to sing his praises, he was sorely disappointed. In fact, his one-time student was rather damning and claimed his teacher had been sacked for 'making rude remarks about girls' and 'strangling' a pupil.

Jim was incandescent, which was understandable since Jonathan's allegations were even less credible than Tony Blair's assertion that Saddam Hussein had WMDs. He took him to court for libel, wielding the sword of truth and the incontrovertible fact that he had retired from teaching, he had not been sacked and he had absolutely, definitely never throttled anyone. Lincoln County Court took one look at his unblemished academic record and ruled in his favour.

Victory, however, was not as sweet as Jim might have envisaged. He was awarded £1,250 in damages, which he described as 'peanuts', and although Friends Reunited were ordered to take down the offending comments, Jim was still not a happy bunny. 'I have dedicated 32 years to education and, if my reputation is only worth £1,250, then that is pathetic,' he said. 'The worst thing of all is that this was permitted by Friends Reunited. They are the real culprits – they have given people *carte blanche*. What was said was not true and I don't see why I should suffer for that. I have had abusive phone calls since it happened.'

The case, though, was a ground-breaker. It was the first time someone had been sued for libel on the Friends Reunited website and, as we now know, the thin edge of the wedge in terms of legal action in response to the deluge of ill-conceived comments on all forms of social media. It is no coincidence that when you go on Twitter today you are simultaneously confronted with a pop-up advertising 'Libel Lawyers 4 U'. We may, of course, have just made that last bit up.

The footnote to our litigious tale was provided in early 2016 when news broke that Friends Reunited was to close and join the technological choir invisible alongside Squarials, Betamax and dial-up Internet access. It was a sad day for the remaining 17 people still using the website but Twitter and Facebook did throw a small party to mark the passing of the once all-conquering behemoth.

GRAND THEFT AUTO

TEXAS, USA, 2005

A teacher's salary is not a king's ransom. Teaching, as they say, is a vocation and if you want to make money hand over fist then you're probably better off joining the rotten ranks of avaricious vultures who grow fat on the misery and misfortune of others. Or bankers as we also call them.

No, teachers don't do it for the money but even the most dedicated educator has to pay the bills somehow. After all, you can only pay the mortgage with hard currency rather than a burning sense of professional pride, and Sainsbury's take a decidedly dim view of anyone who tries to pay for their weekly shopping with the eternal gratitude of a well-educated 12-year-old rather than, say, a major debit or credit card.

Sadly 32-year-old Texas chemistry teacher, Tramesha Lashon Fox, found herself with a few financial problems back in 2005. Specifically she was struggling to meet the repayments on her car – a 2003 Chevrolet Malibu – and was rather scratching her head for a solution. A few sessions as a private tutor could have been the answer to her prayers. A weekend job would have definitely helped boost her finances. She could even have asked her principal for a raise.

Unfortunately Fox had other ideas and decided the best way alleviate her money problems was to set fire to her Chevy and claim the insurance. It wasn't exactly a subtle plan but Fox's mind was made up and she began the search for an accomplice (or indeed accomplices) to actually commit the crime.

It didn't take her long to single out two of her students, Darwin Arias and Roger Luna, as her arsonists. The teenage pair were struggling academically and in a quiet word after class, Fox promised them they'd pass their end-of-term exams with flying colours if they ensured her motor went up in flames.

'The teens initially thought her scheme was a joke, but Fox continued to pursue them,' reported *CBS News*. 'On May 27, the last day of school, the students took the unlocked Chevrolet Malibu from a shopping mall, drove it to a wooded area and set it on fire. Fox reported the theft that day, after already having bought a 2005 Toyota Corolla, investigators said. She owed about $20,000 on the Chevrolet and had been facing repossession.'

When the authorities first suggested to Fox that there was something very fishy about the fire, she claimed it could have been perpetrated by a disgruntled student, but the fire investigators weren't born yesterday and our pyromaniac teacher was soon singing like a canary.

Arias and Luna were both charged with arson and received suspended sentences for their crime, while Fox got 90 days in the Harris County Jail and lost her licence to teach. The fate of her new Toyota Corolla is unknown.

THE BIGGER THE BETTER
INDIA, 2006

Class sizes in our schools have long been a political football in the great education debate. Tony Blair scored a screamer in the top corner in 1997 when he vowed to cut class sizes to a maximum of 30 or under for all five, six and seven-year-olds, helping sweep him into Downing Street, and ever since politicians of all flavours have been vying for our affections and votes by promising our kids will be taught in miniscule classes.

The theory that smaller is better is a pervasive one in modern education and there is an undeniable logic that students will probably learn more if they're surrounded by 20 or so of their peers rather than subsumed in a 100-strong mob. Double maths for 100 kids is after all always likely to degenerate into an exercise in crowd control rather than a detailed study of how to calculate the circumference of a circle.

Not all educators, however, subscribe to the idea that less is more. One such 'splitter' was Indian educator Dr Subramonian who, in 2006, decided he wanted to simultaneously spread his academic gospel to as many students as possible. An expert in computers, the good doctor downloaded some clever software to help him make his dream a reality and, after recruiting some willing pupils and getting them all connected online, he set up a virtual classroom and so registered a new world record for teaching the biggest ever class.

'The largest computer class in multiple locations involved 1,934 participants from 16 different venues worldwide and was organized by Dr Subramonian from Dr R.V. Arts and Science College in Coimbatore, India, for *Guinness World Records* Day on 9 November 2006,' reported the official GWR website. 'The countries involved were: Ecuador, India, Lithuania, Mexico, Nepal, Nigeria, Poland, Taiwan, Thailand and Venezuela.'

Educating nearly 2,000 kids at the same time was certainly no mean feat, not least that nobody lost their Internet connection mid-lesson. Even more remarkably the whole thing was achieved, according to *The Hindu* newspaper, using a dial-up connection.

Dr Subramonian was, of course, delighted by his efforts, but also somewhat chastened after setting the milestone when he realised that he now had 1,934 batches of homework to mark.

'It is not only for the sake of breaking the record, but also to attract the attention of the younger generation towards the teaching profession,' he said, putting a brave face on his catastrophic oversight. 'They should understand that information technology could be put to use for teaching online. Online teaching is keeping in pace with information technology.'

The Doctor's 'mega lesson' was not the first time he had set his sights on creating new world records in the sphere of education. Before his 2006 feat, he earned a place in the Limca *Book of Records* – India's answer to *Guinness World Records* – for the longest continuous lesson, waxing lyrical to a group of students for a staggering 61 hours and 35 minutes. The aforementioned students were permitted regular toilet breaks but that's still surely veering into the realms of child cruelty rather than education.

In 2007 Subramonian really pulled out all the stops when he authored a book with what he hoped would prove the longest ever title. Inspired by J.K. Rowling's *Harry Potter* series, Subramonian's title begins, 'Daniel Radcliffe the story of the not so ordinary boy chosen from …', and after a 1,000 or so more words ends with '… to his ever royal crown of fame.' There's not a single full stop to be seen anywhere in the title and it comes in at 1,022 consecutive and unpunctuated words in total.

'*Harry Potter* is one book that has evoked reading interest among the people,' he told *The Hindu*. 'The character of Harry Potter portrayed by Daniel Radcliffe has had a great influence on the youth. Hence I have written a book on him. His virtues of charity, humility and the urge to excel in life in the face of challenges will help children and youth look up to him as a role model.'

Conducting lessons that last for nearly three days, and penning books with 1,000-word-long titles, however, is unlikely to have made Dr Subramonian much of a role model to his beleaguered pupils.

ACCIDENTAL ACADEMIC ARSON IN AUCKLAND

NEW ZEALAND, 2006

Sadly, it is not unheard of for disgruntled students to vent their anger by setting light to their schools. Acts of arson against school buildings thankfully remain relatively rare, but it's nonetheless a real danger that pupils with an axe to grind will so do via the medium of a can of petrol and a box of matches.

'Arson in schools is a major concern to Fire Protection organisations and the only persons able to resolve the problem is the profession itself,' reads the advice on Fire Safety Advice Centre website. 'School governors, head teachers, school premises managers, LEAs and local authority risk managers are the people who could solve the problem.'

Keeping a close eye on potentially pyromaniacal pupils is sound advice – a flame thrower illicitly stashed in a satchel is usually a dead giveaway – but as this unfortunate tale illustrates, it's not always the students you have to be wary of. Teachers can prove to be a fire risk.

Our flammable educator in question goes by the name of Carl Robson, a teacher at the Drury Christian School, near Auckland in New Zealand. It was a Saturday morning at the end of term and with the school set to open later in the day for a parents' meeting, Carl reported early to light the wood burner to make sure the classroom was nice and toasty when everyone arrived. Unfortunately one of the logs proved too big for the burner and after brushing off the hot embers, Carl returned the oversized piece of fuel to the wood pile at the side of the school and headed home.

At 5.30p.m. Carl was startled by the sound of four fire engines hurtling towards Drury. The log, of course, had smouldered in a sinister fashion all day, and by late afternoon it had burst into flames, igniting the wood pile and in turn the school itself. The quartet of fire engines were too late and his classroom burned to the ground.

It was a devastating blow but there was worse to come. Drury was a small school with just 40 students and Carl's classroom was in fact the *only* classroom. It later emerged the school also had no insurance and the following day, which just happened to be his thirty-second birthday, Carl was forced to sift through the charred remains of the building, a blackened monument to his accidental pyromania.

'As soon as they said "fire", I knew it was my fault', he said. 'It was a stupid mistake. I thought it was out, and I was going to check it but didn't. It was gut wrenching. It wasn't much of a birthday present. It's hard not to blame myself, I do blame myself, but I can't turn back the clock. It's been character building. I can't get down, I've got to get up.'

According to the local fire station chief, Malcolm Brown, such fires were common in the area during the winter months. 'Wood can be burning, even when it looks like it's not,' he said. 'It's a big loss for these people.'

Given that Drury's student body were unexpectedly looking at an extended holiday break as the school was rebuilt, it's debatable whether any of them entirely agreed with him.

TEXTUAL TRANSGRESSIONS

INDIA, 2006

Teachers are often at the mercy of the textbooks with which they are provided. However knowledgeable an educator is on their chosen specialist subject, there are inevitably times when they must instruct students to turn to page 26, begin reading and hope they actually learn something.

Spare a thought, then, for the teachers of India who, over the years, have come to realise that they cannot always rely on the scholastic rigour of the some academic tomes with which they have been supplied. Some of their textbooks are frankly all over the place.

In 2006, for example, schools in the northern state of Rajasthan received books in Hindi for their 14-year-old pupils that contained some rather dubious musings on domestic duties. 'A donkey is like a housewife,' they read. 'It has to toil all day and, like her, may even have to give up food and water. In fact, the donkey is a shade better, for while the housewife may sometimes complain and walk off to her parents' home, you'll never catch the donkey being disloyal to his master.'

The disturbingly patriarchal theme was revisited in 2015 when the Chhattisgarh Board of Secondary Education published a social science textbook in which it was stated that 'working women are one of the causes of unemployment' in India. How they had managed to steal all the men's jobs *and* toil like a donkey at home was not made clear.

Carnivores also got the treatment in 2012 with a national textbook aimed at 11-year-old students, which maintained that people who eat meat 'easily cheat, tell lies, forget promises, are dishonest and tell bad words, steal, fight and turn to violence and commit sex crimes.' Crikey. The book also called for Linda McCartney to be deified. Possibly.

Other errors uncovered in Indian textbooks have been rather more comical than misogynistic or anti *Burger King*, and for a time 50,000 students in the State of Gujarat studying the Second World War were led to believe that it was Japan who had launched a nuclear attack on the US, rather than the other way around. Pupils in Maharashtra meanwhile, to this day, probably still think the Mediterranean is linked to the Red Sea by the 'Sewage Canal'.

The most glaring Indian textbook clanger, however, concerned arguably the country's greatest hero, the one and only Mahatma Gandhi, with one primer contriving to get the date of his untimely assassination wrong. Fortunately for the errant editor of that particular textbook it was Gandhi himself who said 'forgiveness is the attribute of the strong' and he kept his job.

ARE YOU SITTING COMFORTABLY?

BRISTOL, 2006

Employment tribunals brought by disaffected teachers against their schools are usually not a lot of laughs. The need for arbitration between employee and employer does rather suggest a catastrophic breakdown in relations, and when you get the union reps and lawyers involved – belligerent beasts both bred in secret labs specifically for conflict – it can all very quickly descend into the educational equivalent of handbags at dawn.

What is required is a bit of comedy to lighten the mood, or a touch of whimsy to ameliorate the animosity inherent in the proceedings. Or, if you will, a bit of good old-fashioned toilet humour.

And so we come to an employment tribunal in 2006, which saw art teacher and deputy head, Sue Storer, and Bedminster Down Secondary School in Bristol, going head-to-head. Sue was claiming constructive dismissal and sex discrimination, which the school vehemently denied, and you could cut the tension with a blunt knife.

That was until Sue came to discuss one of her greatest grievances against the school. Bedminster Down, she revealed, had made her sit in a chair that repeatedly made farting noises when she sat down, while her male peers had the luxury of silent seats. The tribunal panel desperately tried to stifle their giggles but Sue was not for turning and insisted her apparently flatulent pew was a prime example of the sexism she was forced to endure.

'It was very embarrassing to sit on,' she said. 'It was a regular joke that my chair would make these farting sounds and I regularly had to apologise that it wasn't me, it was my chair. I had specially requested a new chair under health and safety regulations. I say that's discrimination. After 12 months of not receiving a chair, I put in a memo and still didn't receive one. I noticed that my male colleagues had all received an executive-style computer chair.'

It was no laughing matter, though, because Sue was demanding £1 million in lieu of lost earnings and pension payments. The school, however, wasn't going to take that lying (or sitting) down and hit back as headmaster Marius Frank suggested to the tribunal that Sue could have, you know, maybe ordered a fart-free chair for herself. 'I would have expected any member of the leadership team and a deputy head teacher,' he said, 'who has the authority in my absence to run a school, to have the wit and initiative to sort it out.'

The panel retired to consider their verdict in private (and no doubt burst into uncontrolled fits of laughter) but it was bad news for Sue when they returned, ruling that she should really have phoned Rymans and ordered a nice new Eliza Tinsley High Back Executive Chair in faux tan leather. 'The claimant asserts that the provision to her two male colleagues of new chairs ... was discriminatory,' said the tribunal chairman. 'We find that by reason of her status and seniority, she was free to arrange for the purchase of such necessary office equipment ... without prior reference to any of her colleagues.'

Suffice to say Sue needed a bit of a sit down after that disappointing bombshell.

INDECENT EDUCATIONAL EXPOSURE

LONDON, 2006

Teachers getting their kit off in front of students is generally frowned upon. There's nowhere to keep your biros or gold stars, and extensive research has proven the sight of a disrobed educator in the classroom does rather distract pupils from their studies, the logic being a sexagenarian chemistry teacher in the buff is not going to help the kids focus on catalysing hydrogen peroxide with potassium iodide.

Getting naked outside the classroom isn't the path to rapid career progression either. It's OK in the privacy of one's bedroom but parading around in your birthday suit on, say, national television – as Emma Wright of Streatham and Clapham High School in London did – is absolutely, definitely not a good idea.

In her defence, Emma didn't mean to let it all hang out on the TV. The 36-year-old had signed up to appear on a Channel 4 fashion show in the hope of getting a bit of a sartorial makeover, but what with it being the first series of a new show, she didn't know exactly what to expect. She certainly didn't know the show was called *How To Look Good Naked*.

'The programme-makers kept me in the dark,' Emma said. 'I turned up each day not knowing what I was doing. On the day of the photo shoot they literally sat me down and asked if I was prepared to go naked. I agreed but said what I would and wouldn't allow to be shown. I did cry. It was such a momentous occasion.

Emma was probably hoping the show wouldn't be the hit it was to become and few people would see her *au naturel* but it she was, of course, wrong and to compound her embarrassment a 100ft (30.5m) high image of her, sans clothes, was projected onto Waterloo Station to publicise the series, while the Channel 4 website merely added to her discomfort. 'The 36-year-old girls' school teacher Emma Wright should be in her prime,' it read, 'but when it comes to body-loathing, this 1.8m [5ft 11in] tall lass comes top of the class.'

The whole school tuned in to watch Emma's big 'reveal' and parental reaction was mixed. 'I would be appalled at the thought of my pupils' fathers seeing me in my underwear,' one mother fumed. 'She took two weeks off, during which the children had to have a supply teacher. She should have done it in her own time.' Other parents, however, were more supportive. 'Featuring naked on TV may not be the best thing from a career point of view,' said one, 'but it's not going to distract her from being a good teacher.'

Emma faced a nervous wait to see how the school's head and governing body would react to her risqué televisual appearance but she was able to breathe a sigh of relief when they decided that as long as she remained fully clothed in the classroom, and promised to never invite presenter Gok Wan to give the kids fashion tips, they'd let it pass this time.

FACIAL FACSIMILE
SOUTH YORKSHIRE, 2006

The dangers associated with the office Christmas party – liberal lashings of the demon drink and the accounts department's photocopier – are notorious. Emergency departments estimate 50 per cent of patients they treat in December are suffering from shards of glass embedded in the buttocks, while photocopier engineers are rushed off their feet as they race to repair the flood of Xerox machines damaged as a result of the festive frivolities.

The perils of the photocopier are, however, not merely limited to a potential pain in the backside, as unfortunate five-year-old, Luke Wilson, discovered when his teacher at Adwick Washington Infant School in Doncaster, decided she needed a visual aid for a science lesson on the properties of light and dark.

The teacher surveyed the classroom and espied a photocopier, which she deemed the ideal aid to illustrate bright light in action. She photocopied a few of the pupils' hands to kick the lesson off, but when it was unlucky Luke's turn on the machine she decided, for reasons best known to herself, to Xerox his face.

To be fair, the kids thought it was a hoot, but when Luke got home he began to complain his eyes were feeling sore and he had a headache. His parents initially put his symptoms down to tiredness, but when Luke later told them what happened in his science lesson at school, they hit the roof.

'His eyes were still red and itching when he came home from school the next day, and when we asked him if anything had happened he told us his face had been photocopied,' growled his irate dad. 'We couldn't believe what he was saying. We wanted to know why something so stupid had happened and went to the school.

'We saw the photocopy of Luke's head on the classroom wall. We were fuming and informed the police. The teacher didn't have the common sense to realise what she was doing was dangerous. It was totally irresponsible, a stupid thing to do by someone in charge of young children. Surely she should have realised how dangerous it was. Luke could have been left with serious eye damage or even blinded.'

Luke was hastily bundled off to the local hospital where he was diagnosed with allergic conjunctivitis, caused by exposure to strong light, and although he mercifully suffered no long-term problems after his photocopier portrait, his teacher was far from in the clear as the police launched an investigation. After extensive research of the Policeman's Handbook, however, the long arm of the law could find not anywhere where it said it was illegal to photocopy a minor's face and she was let off without charge.

SEMI-NAKED
ANNIVERSARY MAYHEM
NOTTINGHAM, 2007

Not unlike nature's attitude to vacuums, teachers abhor birthdays. Not their own obviously, there's usually a whip-round in the staff room that yields a cake from the local supermarket and a bottle of something to liven up lunchtime, but a student's big day is an altogether different beast.

Teachers, of course, pretend to be enchanted by the fact Timmy has reached the age he can legally play *Call of Duty*, or Jennifer can get a One Direction tattoo without parental permission, but the truth is that birthdays are disruptive and tend to upset the fragile ecosystem that is the classroom. Teenage anniversaries are the worst of the lot.

And so it proved at Arnold Hill School in Nottingham when a drama teacher prepared for a lesson with her class. She was about to start exploring the arguments surrounding the great method versus character acting debate when a mother popped her head around the door, informed her it was her not-so-little boy's sixteenth birthday, and that she had arranged a surprise for him. Our drama teacher sighed wearily, dutifully replied, 'How delightful,' and steeled herself for the imminent arrival of an avalanche of balloons, party poppers and pizza.

No one expected a stripper to turn up. Well you wouldn't, would you? 'It happened just before lunch when we were in drama class, discussing our GCSE coursework,' revealed one of the class. 'The teacher suddenly announced

'Something is about to happen'. Then a woman in a very short skirt walked in dressed as a police officer. She asked the lad to stand up, which he did, and told him he had been a very naughty boy because he hadn't been doing his homework.

'Then she put on some Britney Spears music and got out a collar and lead from her bag and told him to put them on. No one could believe it. Next she ordered him to get on all fours, led him around the classroom and hit him 16 times – one for each year – on the bottom with her whip.'

'Then she took off some clothes until she was down to her bra and pants, pulled out some cream, put it on her buttocks and told him to rub it in. To be fair to the teacher, you could tell she was just stunned – and when the cream came out she told the stripper, "That's it, that's enough".'

The cacophony of boos from the male members of the class was deafening but the show did not go on. The embarrassed birthday boy beat a hasty retreat from the classroom, the 'performer' packed her 'equipment' and left, and the school began the post mortem into what on earth had just happened.

The drama teacher was quickly absolved of blame, which rather disappointed the NUT who hadn't had a strike for ages. The mother also pleaded innocence, insisting she had booked a gorillagram not a stripper, and the finger of suspicion quickly pointed to Nottingham-based Sam's Entertainment, the firm that had taken the original booking. 'If this happened in front of the kids then it's outrageous,' said someone from the company, who may or may not have been Sam. 'We get kids ringing up now and again, but we always say no.'

The mystery of the misunderstanding was never satisfactorily solved, despite an investigation by Nottinghamshire County Council, but Arnold Hill did notice a significant spike in the numbers of male pupils signing up for drama the following year.

SANTA'S SUDDEN EXPOSURE

GREATER MANCHESTER, 2008

The last few days of term before Christmas are a magical time at most schools. The children's excitement at the orgy of presents to follow is inescapable, the final, feverish preparations for the Nativity Play create a suitably festive atmosphere, and with teachers having invariably abandoned trigonometry and comprehension in favour of a *Frozen* DVD, it's a fun time for all.

The Christmas spirit was, however, rather conspicuous by its absence at Blackshaw Lane Primary School in Greater Manchester in 2008. The kids were, of course, as hyper as ever, but the arrival of a curmudgeonly supply teacher put a rather spectacular dampener on proceedings.

The unnamed teacher was taking charge of a class when she became infuriated by the seven and eight-year-olds' constant chattering about their impending Christmas holidays. She was determined to restore order, but rather than employing a time-honoured distraction tactic or even sending the ringleader to the naughty corner, she went nuclear and told the kids that Father Christmas didn't exist.

The stunned silence that briefly followed before the collective flood of tears certainly quietened things down for a bit but the chorus of parental disapproval was louder than any of the noise the kids had generated.

'My son came home and said that his substitute teacher had told the class that Santa doesn't exist and it's your mum and dad that put out presents for them,' fumed one understandably irate father. 'Apparently, they were all talking about Christmas and being a bit rowdy. She just came straight out with it.'

'My lad was nearly in tears and so was everyone else in the class – especially as it was so close to Christmas. I thought it was wrong. He was distraught about it. He's only seven years old and it's part of the magic of Christmas to him.'

'We told him that she did not believe in Father Christmas because of her religion and he's fine now. I found it shocking. She has done it maliciously. A lot of parents were disgusted and complained to the school. If she was a regular teacher then I think a lot more would have been done.'

Headmistress Angel McCormick wasn't happy either. 'I would like to apologise to all of our parents and pupils for any upset that has been caused,' she said. 'I have spoken to the supply agency concerned and have completed a complaints form. I am pleased to say that the children are unscathed and are back on the right track thanks to the professionalism of our resident staff and the lovely snow we experienced last week. They really are looking forward to the magic of Christmas morning and have watched their Christmas production and written letters to Santa.'

For any younger readers of this book, we'd like to make it crystal clear that Father Christmas is, of course, very real indeed and is going to find out who's been naughty or nice. So behave yourselves.

STRIPPED FOR ACTION
SUFFOLK, 2008

Grabbing your pupils' attention is an essential part of the job as a teacher. The classroom is no place for the shy or retiring and every successful educator must learn the techniques for getting their students to sit up nicely and concentrate.

In the past, some teachers were passionate advocates of the 'blackboard eraser as an improvised projectile' method of focusing young minds, but that has rather gone out of fashion due to woeful aerodynamic qualities of modern Smartboard Erasers and cautionary advice from both the police and social services. For the same reason, a short, sharp swing of a long ruler is also very much frowned upon these days.

Up-to-date alternatives to get pupils to behave and listen are all about 'engaging' with them and although they lack somewhat in terms of shock and awe, not to mention the satisfaction of watching kids duck for cover as the eraser flies menacingly through the air, any method that successfully allows teachers to teach cannot be sniffed at.

It was, however, a very different technique that was deployed by an English supply teacher in Suffolk in 2008 as he battled to get his new charges to learn something. As is the fate of many supply teachers, our unnamed educator was struggling to get the teenage students of Sudbury Upper School and Arts College to pay attention in class, but rather than resort to shouting or physical violence via the medium of office equipment, he took a bizarre approach which involved stripping to the waist and forcing the kids to look at his less-than-buff body.

'Kids were playing up in class and his way of dealing with it was to tell everyone to be quiet or he would take his shirt off and show his man boobs,' said one student after witnessing the surreal but mercifully only partial striptease. 'He was quite overweight and it was a sight that nobody really wanted to see. Everyone thought he was joking and people carried on messing around but then he really did take his shirt off. It was quite shocking.'

'It was hilarious,' added another one of the pupils. 'People were goading him saying, "I bet you haven't got muscles". He told us all, "I'll show you" and started taking off his shirt. We all thought he was pretending but he took his shirt off and started flexing his muscles. Then he said, "Look, I told you." He put his shirt back on but he was still buttoning it up when he was teaching. Everyone was killing themselves laughing.'

Unfortunately for our disrobing teacher, his antics were captured on a camera phone, and before the day was out a 53-second clip of his impromptu strip, in which one female student could clearly be heard wailing 'Oh my God!', was doing the rounds at school. It wasn't long, of course, before it was uploaded to YouTube under the heading 'Teacher Strip' with the accompanying caveat 'make sure your not eating when ur wachin this'.

If our risqué English teacher was appalled with the spelling and grammar on display, it was nothing compared to the headmaster's displeasure after watching the clip and our stripper was promptly escorted off the premises and told in no uncertain terms never to darken the school's door again. A few days later Suffolk County Council confirmed that he would not be allowed to teach in any of its 357 schools.

Ironically the incident came just a month after Ofsted had

inspected Sudbury Upper and reported that 'most [pupils] behave well but there are occasions, especially in lessons, where there is inconsistency in the quality of teaching and management of behaviour, when some students are not engaged in learning.'

The school's pass rate for Pole Dancing Studies came in for particular criticism.

A MAGICAL
CLASSROOM MISHAP

FLORIDA, USA, 2008

The media is frequently accused of hyperbole, misrepresentation and, you know, just making things up. Anything for a good headline, the critics argue, and it is sadly true that the press have been known from time to time to sacrifice the truth at the sordid altar of sensationalism.

The Fifth Estate's penchant for not letting the facts get in the way of a story was very much in evidence over in the US in 2008, when news broke of a supply teacher in Florida who had just been sacked. In ordinary circumstances hardly headline news, but when it emerged the educator in question had apparently been given his marching orders after practising black magic in the classroom, the media were all over it like a rash.

'Florida Substitute Teacher Fired, Accused of Wizardry' ran the headline on the *Fox News* website. 'A Florida teacher may have to pull an unemployment check out of his hat,' continued the story, 'after performing magic in front of students, according to reports. Jim Piculas said he made a toothpick disappear and reappear in front of students at the Rushe Middle School in Land O'Lakes, Florida. He said he later got a call from the supervisor of teachers, saying he had been accused of wizardry.'

It's certainly a bizarre reason to get the sack and unsurprisingly the story had real legs. The following day it was featured heavily on television throughout America, with political commentator Keith Olbermann mocking the local education authorities on his show on the MSNBC channel for their kneejerk decision to sack Piculas. 'Most of Florida is in the Eastern time zone,' he joked. 'But apparently Land O'Lakes is one of those pockets that uses its own clock. Their time zone is apparently the Middle Ages.'

All was not quite as it seemed, however. It later transpired that the first person to use the word 'wizardry' in connection with the story was Piculas himself when he phoned up his local radio station to publicise his plight and, despite suddenly becoming public enemy number one, the local Pasco County education board was adamant he'd got the boot for his failure to follow prescribed lesson plans, his use of bad language and his decision to put one of the students in charge of the class. They didn't, they insisted, have any problem with him impersonating Harry Potter even if it was sad behaviour for a 48-year-old.

'There were several compelling reasons for the dismissal,' wrote Superintendent Heather Fiorentino. 'None of which were even remotely related to "wizardry", as was suggested in the news accounts.' It took a few days for the media to tire of the story, but when they did the 'truth' began to slowly emerge, and people realised that incompetence rather than the dark arts were to blame for Piculas' sudden unemployment.

'The teacher was very smart,' said Sree Sreenivasan, a professor of new media at the Columbia University School of Journalism. 'It was in his interest to spin it the way he did. That's a headline I would click and read.'

It's unclear whether Piculas was able to 'magic up' another job for himself after all the misleading furore but we can safely assume he didn't hear back after sending his CV to Hogwarts.

LEONORA'S
LITERARY LAPSE
WEST YORKSHIRE, 2008

Problem pupils inhabit almost every school and academic opinion tends to be divided on whether the carrot or the stick approach is the best solution for those troubled students who don't exactly embrace their education.

Those who advocate the carrot argue it's a healthy, nutritious snack packed full of Vitamin C. Hang on, that's not right, that's vegetarians. No, the fans of the educational carrot believe that only by encouragement rather than censure can difficult students be helped to realise their full, albeit well disguised potential, while devotees of the stick insist it's the only language teenage tearaways understand.

Former secondary school teacher Leonora Rustamova was firmly in the former camp. Affectionately dubbed 'Miss Rusty' by her pupils, Leonora had five 16-year-old boys in her class who had been effectively written off after years of bad behaviour at Calder High School in West Yorkshire, but she refused to give up on the problematic teenagers.

She hit on the idea of writing a book, a fictionalised account of the boys' lives. The deal was she would read them a new chapter every Friday afternoon if the lads got through the week without any of them being excluded from class and her story proved so gripping that their behaviour and academic performance improved significantly.

Mischievously Leonora called her book *Stop! Don't Read This!* and as the academic year drew to a close, she had a few copies printed for the boys as a leaving present. The teenagers were delighted but not everyone at Calder High was as enamoured by her literary efforts, and in January 2008 she was summoned to the headmaster's office, formally suspended and escorted from the school premises.

The problem was that Miss Rusty was deemed to have been a little too risqué. Specifically the powers-that-be were displeased with the plot of *Stop! Don't Read This!* – a story of five boys who thwart a drugs gang's attempts to use their school as store for their narcotics – and they were absolutely livid that Leonora alluded to one of the 'fictional' boy's sexual fantasies about her and referred to another two of the teenagers as 'looking like two gorgeous Mr Gay UK finalists.' She also used her pupils' real names in the book and once the most conservative elements of the school had stopped choking on their cornflakes, all hell broke loose.

The five boys, their families and many of the school's other students protested in support of Leonora, taking to the local radio station to decry her treatment, but the head, governors and local authority were deaf to their anger and after a disciplinary hearing in 2009, Miss Rusty was sacked.

'It was baffling, utterly baffling. I still feel as though I am in some kind of dual reality,' she said in an interview. 'They were a really difficult-to-reach group: spirited, very intimidating to teach at first. We were all struggling to find a way of getting through to them and most of the time they were getting excluded. These were the kind of kids who really are cynical about education because they have never been engaged by it.'

'It boosted their self-esteem, it engaged them. We were having conversations and discussions. For a group of boys like this, that was incredible. I thought it would be a lovely gesture to have it printed for them when they left school. We keep in touch and they like to joke that I spent so much time getting them to avoid the dole queue and now it's me that's on it, not them. I can't regret the book because of the effect it had on the students. I regret my career coming crashing down.'

Miss Rusty, however, had the last laugh after losing her job. As well as teaching creative studies at the University of Huddersfield and working with adults with learning difficulties at a college in Leeds, she reinvented herself as a professional writer. So should you type her name into any well-know online book retailer, you will discover Leonora is in fact the author of *Yorkshire's Strangest Tales*, an old title from this very series of books. 'It is something good,' she said, 'that came out of a hideous sacking experience.'

Of course none of the beastly business would have unfolded in the first place if whoever snitched on Leonora had just taken *Stop! Don't Read This!* at face value.

A RAPID GETAWAY
WEST VIRGINIA, USA, 2008

Missing classes is a bad thing. Absenteeism is the sworn enemy of a good education and pupils these days must have an authenticated doctor's note, written in triplicate in blood, before they can even dream about taking a day off with illness. Parents who don't ensure their kids are in school are subject to the attentions of a secretive branch of MI6 with full powers of detention and torture.

Teachers failing to turn up to teach is equally unacceptable. As we all know, classrooms have rather a tendency to get a bit *Lord of the Flies* if the students are left to their own devices and there's no responsible adult *in situ*, while the chances of any student actually passing an exam or two are virtually non-existent without the reassuring presence of a qualified educator.

But like anyone, teachers sometimes have to take time off due to sickness. Sometimes they really *are* poorly but sometimes, as in any other profession, it's no more than a wafer thin excuse for an unscheduled day off.

When art teacher Melissa Brown called in sick to her job at Stonewall Jackson Middle School in West Virginia in 2008, the principal had to reluctantly wish her better soon and hastily organise cover. When Melissa phoned the following week and said she was feeling under the weather again, the principal muttered darkly before summoning another supply teacher.

Melissa, of course, was in perfect health both times, as her boss suspected, but rather than using her two sickies as duvet days, complete with the box set of *Sex and the City* and a bottle of Chardonnay, she was out and about. More specifically, she was out helping her brother Jeremy rob two local banks.

Jezza did the actual gun-wielding, stick-up end of the crime while Melissa kept their motor, a Chevrolet Cavalier if you're interested, running in readiness for a quick getaway. First they knocked over the City National Bank and a week later targeted the First Sentry Bank, making off with the less-than-princely sum of $6,561 from the two robberies combined, but were pulled over by the long arm of the law just minutes after the second heist.

The police began the interrogation and it quickly emerged the brother and sister duo were responsible for both bank jobs. 'It was determined that the details surrounding both robberies were identical,' said local officer Steve Cooper. 'After the interview process, the suspects implicated themselves in both robberies.'

Melissa was a picture of contrition at her trial, apologising to her family and her erstwhile pupils, but the judge was unimpressed and sentenced our blagging art teacher to 37 months imprisonment.

Her former employers were understandably dismayed at all the negative publicity they received after Melissa's crime spree but made rather a horrible hash of the subsequent damage limitation. 'We've got bigger problems in our school,' said one board member, 'than having one teacher who drove a getaway car in a bank heist.' Unsurprisingly it was not a quote that made the Stonewall Jackson Middle School's next promotional brochure.

THE BABY-FACED BOSS
INDIA, 2009

One of the first signs you're getting old is when you find yourself remarking how young policemen are looking these days. Other indications you're no longer a spring chicken include an inability to successfully navigate the myriad of remotes in the living room to turn the TV on, realising you've got absolutely no idea what a terabyte is and finally discovering to your horror that you're not even in the easy listening target demographic any more.

The policeman analogy also applies to education, and teachers worldwide were left feeling absolutely ancient when news emerged in 2009, that a 16-year-old in India had just been appointed the headmaster of his local school. Admittedly, the teenager in question got the job at a school he had set up himself, but it was nonetheless a remarkable story which proved the old adage that if you're good enough you're old enough.

Our youthful educator goes by the name of Babar Ali. A student at the prestigious Raj Govinda School in West Bengal, Babar travelled 6 miles (9.7km) each way each day, walking for much of the journey, from his village of Mursidabad to the college, but with many poorer children in the area receiving no formal education at all, he was one of the lucky ones.

The lack of academic opportunities for his peers did not sit easy with Babar, and so at the age of just nine he decided to start sharing what he'd learned at school with his friends every afternoon. At the start it was only a few of the children from the village, but after he set up an improvised teaching area in the backyard of his parent's house, his 'school' grew and by 2009 the teenager was the headmaster of a thriving, free educational establishment with 800 pupils.

'In the beginning I was just play-acting, teaching my friends, but then I realised these children will never learn to read and write if they don't have proper lessons', he told the BBC. 'It just occurred to me why not teach them what I learned in my class. It's my duty to educate them, to help our country build a better future. Our area is economically deprived. Without this school many kids wouldn't get an education, they'd never even be literate.

'We still needed books, so I went to the parents and guardians of all my students and collected rice from them. I sold that and bought alphabet books for the students. Meanwhile, my teachers in school were happy that I was doing this. My father too came around and donated money to my school. Of course, my mother had always supported me and she continued doing that in her own way.'

Babar's school is still going strong today, and in 2015 work started on construction of a new building to house his college, funded in part by charitable denotation and in part by the cash he won for his altruistic educational work. 'I realised that I needed a school building but it was becoming difficult to get the funds for a building,' he said, 'I had already bought a wasteland near my house with the Real Hero prize money that I had received, but did not at first have enough to construct a building.'

Babar's selfless example is indeed an inspirational one and proves that the Greek philosopher Diogenes was absolutely spot-on when he observed that 'The foundation of every state is the education of its youth.' Or indeed Mark Twain's observation that 'Age is an issue of mind over matter. If you don't mind, it doesn't matter.'

THE CASE OF THE DUBIOUS DVD

CALIFORNIA, USA, 2009

Modern film editing technology is a splendid thing and thanks to the wonder of all sorts of electronic wizardry and frightfully clever software, we can all now live out our Steven Spielberg or Francis Ford Coppola fantasies, cutting and splicing our amateur homemade movies to within an inch of their lives.

The revolution in editing has been particularly embraced by teachers, who can now take the traditionally disjointed, out-of-focus footage of the school play, or the school trip to the British Museum and produce something rather special indeed. The new, readily available software can cover a multitude of sins, and such is the quality attainable that many schools are now regularly rinsing poor parents for a few extra quid by selling DVDs of the everything from the acclaimed class assembly on global warming, to the less well received presentation on gender issues in *Dora the Explorer*.

It is, however, prudent to thoroughly check such DVDs before they are sent out. Nobody wants the children to be exposed to anything inappropriate, do they?

It's a salutary lesson embarrassingly learned by American teacher, Crystal Defanti of the Isabelle Jackson Elementary School in California, when she sat down at her PC at the end of term in 2009, booted up Microsoft's Movie Maker (or whatever it was) and set about compiling a DVD of her pupils' best moments from the academic year.

Crystal was initially pleased with her efforts but her happiness rapidly turned to despair when she received a call from one of her pupil's parents. Did Crystal realise she had accidentally included a rather revealing and extremely explicit six-second clip of herself on a sofa? A clip of her *in solo flagrante* so to speak. Enjoying an intimate feminine moment. Horrified, Crystal hurriedly checked the DVD and discovered she had indeed accidentally edited in some footage from what we can only assume was marked up as her 'personal' folder.

There was nothing for it but to make a series of increasingly hysterical calls to other parents, urging them to destroy their DVDs and under no circumstances let little Billy or Tammy watch it. Sadly, Crystal was not wholly successful with her desperate attempts to put the cinematic genie back in the bottle, and some of her class of ten and 11-year-olds did indeed see her in all her glory.

'It goes from my son, straight to her on the couch', revealed one father, who wisely decided to remain anonymous. 'My son's reaction was, "Dad, is that Ms Defanti?" We were up till midnight doing the birds and the bees. All she could say was that it was a horrible mix up. Maybe offer some sort of counselling for my children [would be appropriate], asking me how my children are doing.'

All that was left to unfold was whether the 29-year-old was going to keep her job. The mood amongst the parents was predominantly forgiving, particularly among the dads, while legal experts said it would be difficult to sack her for what was clearly an honest if rather graphic mistake. 'It's felony stupid, but it's not a crime,' Ken Rosenfeld told *CBS News*. 'Is it something that she should be disciplined for? Absolutely, but fired for? She didn't intend for this to happen.'

Crystal wasn't let go by the school but it was made, ahem, crystal clear that she wouldn't be let anywhere near an Isabelle Jackson Elementary DVD in the future. She was also advised to avoid at all costs Googling her own name for the next ten years or so and going anywhere near YouTube.

STEVE'S SARTORIAL SLIP
GREATER MANCHESTER, 2010

Schools have a uniform policy for a reason. It's not always entirely clear what that reason is, but it's got something to do with focusing on French rather than the latest fashions, and students worrying about their academic work rather than what to wear. It's also all about crushing any sense of individuality and discouraging independent thought, although that bit might not really be true.

How to dress appropriately for the academic environment is an important lesson for all students, lest they spend the majority of their teenage years in detention, but sometimes it is the teachers who rather let the side down in a sartorial sense.

Steve Smith did just that when he turned up for a day's work as music supply teacher at swanky Greater Manchester grammar school St Ambrose College. Steve had wisely left his *Napalm Death* T-shirt at home in favour of a clean shirt, and was sporting his best suede loafers, but the 52-year-old had neglected to wear a tie. His oversight displeased one of the school's deputy heads and the pair became embroiled in a heated exchange over what was the correct attire for St Ambrose's.

'He demanded to know where my tie was,' said Steve. 'I explained I had never worn a tie for 15 or 16 years. He said I wasn't dressed professionally and ridiculed me in front of all the staff. He told me to tuck my shirt in. It was a smart dress shirt which was not cut to be tucked in. I dress extremely well.

'Then he went to get me a vulgar representation of a tie. It was a piece of brown cloth shoved in front of my nose that had no aesthetic value to the suit I was wearing. I refused and I complained. He announced to the staff that "Mr Smith is now leaving because he does not want to wear a tie" and I was thrown out.

'I was smartly presented. There were other male members of staff there that morning who were unshaven, wore unpolished shoes and shabby shirts. I couldn't believe the way I was treated. I was angry and upset, surprised and dumbfounded. I'm very experienced and I've never been treated this way. I've never worn a tie. I don't feel comfortable wearing one. I don't think that's a representation of someone's professional values or integrity.'

Steve decided to get legal on St Ambrose. He lodged a case at an industrial tribunal claiming breach of conduct and sexual discrimination on the grounds female members of staff were not required to wear ties, brown and vulgar or otherwise. He even had UK TV's self-appointed style gurus Trinny and Susannah on standby as expert sartorial witnesses for the hearing. Perhaps.

A week before the tribunal was scheduled to start, the school offered Steve £150 – his fee for the aborted day's teaching – as a goodwill gesture to make all the unpleasantness go away. There's no such thing as a free lunch, however, and as part of the deal they demanded Steve stop banging on about the incident to the press. He refused the offer but agreed to drop the tribunal proceedings, reasoning that it had all got rather out of hand and his favourite show, *What Not to Wear,* was about to start on BBC Two.

DON'T LOOK BACK IN ANGER

QATAR, 2010

Surely there cannot be a teacher who has not, at some time during their educational career, wished that they had eyes in the back of their heads. Just imagine the benefits of 360-degree vision in the classroom and the ability to keep even the most unruly of students under constant ocular surveillance. The seditious little monsters wouldn't know what hit them, while a teacher with such powers of wraparound observation would be unlikely to ever be caught out even by the stealthiest head teacher.

The next best thing of course would be a video camera on the back of the head, and in 2010 an Iraqi professor by the name of Wafaa Bilal from the Arab Museum of Modern Art in Qatar, became the teaching profession's answer to RoboCop when he voluntarily had a camera surgically implanted in his head. The painful-sounding procedure involved Wafaa having a titanium plate attached to his cranium onto which a small camera was bolted.

He dubbed the experiment the *3rdi* and explained what he was trying to achieve on his website. 'Technically, the *3rdi* is an automatic photographic apparatus that is comprised of three different components,' he wrote. 'A small digital camera permanently, surgically mounted to the back of my head with a USB connection, a lightweight laptop which I carry on my body connected to the camera with a USB cable, and a 3G wireless connection to access the internet.'

'The *3rdi* is just such a platform for the telling and retelling of another story. A camera temporarily implanted on the back of my head, it spontaneously and objectively captures the images – one per minute – that make up my daily life, and transmits them to a website for public consumption.

'The *3rd*i arises from a need to objectively capture my past as it slips behind me from a non-confrontational point of view. It is anti-photography, decoded, and will capture images that are denoted rather than connoted, a technological-biological image. This will be accomplished by the complete removal of my hand and eye from the photographic process, circumventing the traditional conventions of traditional photography or a disruption in the photographic program.'

Whatever, Wafaa. What about the surveillance implications? How many mischievous but unsuspecting undergraduates did you catch flicking you the V-sign when your back was turned in class with your ingenious Bond-esque gadget? None, because sadly there were two major problems with the *3rdi* that rather undermined its potential as a state-of-art teaching aid.

The first setback was the fact he wasn't actually allowed to use his potentially revolutionary device on campus. Student privacy concerns forbade it and Wafaa was compelled to cover up his camera in class. Secondly, and he perhaps should have seen this coming, having a titanium plate surgically implanted his head did rather hurt a touch. The experiment was scheduled to last a full year but Wafaa threw in the towel after little more than a month because he was in constant pain.

So unfortunately the first attempt to give teachers an electronic edge on the front line of the classroom was a failure, but Wafaa's work has surely paved the way for another innovative educator to take the next step. The benefits are obvious and who knows, in a few decades hence, teachers need never fear again when they turn their backs on an unruly class to write out the periodic table, or the first lines of 'I Wandered Lonely as a Cloud', on the blackboard.

MARION'S BUNNY BLUES
GERMANY, 2010

The past has an unerring knack of catching up with the best of us. Like a dog trying to outrun its own tail, there's just no escape from it, and irrespective of how much distance we attempt to put between ourselves and the things which we wish to forget, sooner or later the past will inevitably catch up with us like Usain Bolt being chased by the Grim Reaper.

And so it was for a 60-year-old secondary-school teacher in Germany in 2010, known for legal reasons (more of which presently) only as Marion V., who switched schools but sadly failed to leave behind a debilitating phobia that left her rather vulnerable to the more waggish members of the student body.

Poor old Marion suffered from leporiphobia. If your Latin is a bit rusty, that's a morbid fear of rabbits and Marion's distaste for the little fellas with the big ears had already caused something of a stir at her previous school in 2008, when a cruel pupil had spread rumours about her phobia and told stories of how she would she burst into tears and flee the classroom if she saw a picture of a rabbit or someone even said the word.

She hoped a change of scenery and a new job teaching German and geography in the town of Vechta in Lower Saxony would put all the unseemly business behind her, but she hadn't reckoned on one of her former students called Kim heading in the same direction and bringing with her tales of Marion's unfortunate leporiphobia. It wasn't long before another pupil had drawn a rabbit on the blackboard to test the truth of Kim's tales, an image which sent the distressed teacher racing from the classroom.

Marion, however, wasn't going to take it lying down and took Kim to court for defamation. 'The plaintiff, a teacher, teaches the accused pupil at a high school in Vechta and claims the pupil drew rabbits on the blackboard of the classroom and told fellow pupils the teacher was afraid of rabbits and "flips out" when she sees a rabbit,' the court said in a statement. 'The teacher demands that the accused refrains in future from drawing rabbits on the blackboard, claiming that she, the teacher, is afraid of rabbits and flips out at the sight of them.'

It certainly wasn't your average, run-of-the mill legal wrangle but Kim refused to be cowed. 'I didn't draw the rabbit,' the 16-year-told told the judge. 'I know the teacher from my previous school where she also gave lessons. All I did was tell another pupil that she used to run out of the classroom whenever she saw a drawing of a rabbit.' Another of Marion's students added, 'We did it for fun and out of curiosity. We wanted to see if she would really freak out.'

The case made national news in Germany. Kim was facing a €5,000 fine if found guilty of defamation but her defence came up with a cunning legal manoeuvre – they argued she couldn't possibly have defamed her teacher because it was patently obvious that Marion bloody well was terrified of the friends of Cottontail, Roger, Bugs and the ensemble cast of *Watership Down*. Marion, they insisted, was a stone cold leporiphobe.

In a rare case of judicial common sense, the judge had to agree and Kim was exonerated. Sadly for Marion, the cat if not the rabbit was out of the bag after all the publicity, and there was now not a single school in Germany in which she could teach without fear of a cuddly Flopsy or a copy of *The Tale of Benjamin Bunny* making an appearance on her desk on a daily basis.

WOE FOR UOW

WALES AND MALAYSIA, 2010

You just can't trust airports these days. They're shameless lying charlatans, you know. Utterly untrustworthy. We're talking, of course, about the modern trend to be rather creative but bloody misleading when it comes to the naming of our aerial transport hubs.

Take Robin Hood Airport for example. The name suggests you might reasonably expect to catch a glimpse of the famed Sherwood Forest as you land, but given that it's in Yorkshire and not actually Nottingham, you're far more likely to see a carpeting of flat caps, whippets and Geoffrey Boycott. Similarly, when you touch down at London Southend you've got more chance of getting your feet wet in the North Sea rather than catching a glimpse of the fountains of Trafalgar Square, seeing as the capital is a whopping great 42 miles (67.6km) to the west of where you've just landed.

The educational equivalent of this erroneous naming is the growing number of British universities and colleges offering courses through third parties. Fancy a degree but can't be bothered to actually head to the city where the university in question is based? No problem, you can now complete the course hundreds, if not thousands, of miles away safe in the knowledge that your qualification has been 'certified' by the 'parent' uni.

This trend for third party education is not without its dangers, however, and the University of Wales was left with lashes of educational egg on its face in 2010 after teaming up with a colourful character over in Malaysia, a mere 6,700 miles (10,782km) away.

The deal was simple. The Fazley International College in Kuala Lumpur would offer students degree courses from the Principality's finest academic establishment and the University of Wales would keep a proprietorial eye on proceedings. You know, ensuring scholastic standards were maintained and all that.

The problem was the UOW weren't exactly thorough in their background checks on the head of the college, one Fazley Yaakob. That at least solves the mystery of where the college got its name, but certainly doesn't shed any light on why the University decided a chap whose day job was as a Malaysian pop star, releasing four hit albums, was the right man to run the satellite school.

To be fair Yaakob did have a masters degree and doctorate in business administration on his CV and not many pop stars can say that. Unfortunately his qualifications were from the European Business School Cambridge, an offshoot of the Irish International University and totally, irredeemably bogus. He'd bought 'em off the Internet.

It was red faces all round at the University of Wales when it emerged Yaakob was a fraud after a BBC investigation, and he quickly resigned as the college's executive director. 'We are not happy about what is happening,' said UOW Professor Nigel Palastanga. 'We are dealing with it and will deal with it very thoroughly and will learn lessons from what has happened.'

The first lesson, one suspects, is not to allow a charlatan on the other side of the world to offer education on your behalf.

The scandal may have rocked the UOW but Yaakob didn't let the grass grow under his feet for long, and a couple of years later was crowned the inaugural winner of Malaysia's version of *Celebrity Masterchef*. The judges were apparently particularly impressed with his delicious Welsh rarebit.

PAPER MONEY
FLORIDA, USA, 2011

Money has always been a hot topic in the world of education. Teachers' salaries, how much government spends on the academic infrastructure and whose turn it is to pay for the coffee and cookies for the staff room, these are all financial issues which are invariably significant in the scholastic sphere.

Matters monetary were also very much top of the agenda at Charlotte High School in Florida in 2011, but sadly the cash in question was of the elicit nature, and this was not one of the teaching profession's finest hours.

The educator at the centre of this particular tale was maths teacher Jeff Spires. Unfortunately Jeff found himself in pecuniary difficulties and facing bankruptcy, and when one of his lottery scratch cards failed to yield the windfall he craved, he decided desperate times demanded desperate remedies.

And so Jeff subtly let it be known around school that should any of his pupils, say, paper clip a few dollars to the back of their maths tests or homework, they might well find they were pleasantly surprised with their subsequent marks. Yep, Jeff was selling better grades for cold, hard currency. An eleventh-grade pupil apparently attached $70 to his paper and saw his mark rise from a C to a B while a senior student stumped up $30 to miraculously transform his B into an A. The first kid was clearly fleeced but you get the picture.

The scam was working a treat for a while but the wheels came off in spectacular style when one of his charges took to the ratemyteacher.com website to leave a review of Jeff's class and his dastardly educational subterfuge. 'Awesome teacher,' wrote the student. 'Bought grade for 10 bucks and a car wash coupon. The coupon was expired but he did not notice.'

Charlotte High School was furious and Jeff was promptly suspended without pay pending an investigation. The educational secret police soon bundled him into a darkened room and demanded an explanation. 'That's what I don't know – why,' he said. 'Maybe I see the kids are as desperate as I am.'

Jeff jumped before he was pushed, resigning from his job the following month. His licence to teach was revoked while the Office of Professional Practices at the Florida Department of Education confirmed he would never darken another classroom in the Sunshine State again. 'It's disrespectful for the kids who work hard to earn grades and for teachers who set high standards for kids,' fumed Mike Riley, a spokesman for Charlotte County Public Schools. 'It's about ethics, it's about character. We hold our teachers to a high standard and that's disappointing.'

Jeff's erstwhile pupils weren't impressed either. 'If he really needed extra money, you only work six hours a day here, get a night job or something,' said one outraged student. 'Even if you're going through a hard time, it's still wrong of you to take money, especially from students.'

To clarify the rules for any recently qualified teachers, accepting an apple from a pupil is perfectly acceptable. Taking £100, a new Rolex and the details of their current account is not.

AN EXPLOSIVE SOLUTION
COLORADO, USA, 2011

What teacher hasn't been rudely woken by the sound of their alarm of a morning and groaned audibly at the prospect of the day ahead exploring the genius of Hamlet's soliloquy with a group of disinterested teenagers, stopping a nursery-school class from squabbling over the last copy of *The Very Hungry Caterpillar*, or explaining for a third time to a group of 13-year-olds in a maths focus group that their compasses are not, under absolutely any circumstances, to be used to create DIY tattoos.

Yes, even the most dedicated and passionate teacher occasionally yearns for an impromptu day off, but the vast majority, albeit reluctantly, gird their loins and head off to school nonetheless. It's a tough job but someone's got to do it.

Part-time sports teacher Jennifer Gomes definitely didn't want to put in a shift at the Escuela de Guadallupe School in Denver in 2011. She had, to be fair, managed to drag herself out of bed, but when confronted by the mental image of spending her day surrounded sweaty and surly school children, she snapped and decided there was no way she was going to work.

But how to manufacture a cherished day off? Call in sick? Invent a death in the family? Claim her religion was Jediism and say it was the sacred Obi-Wan Kenobi Day? No, Jennifer took rather more drastic measures to ensure she would not be in gainful employment that particular day – or as it transpired any other day in the future – and pinned a handwritten note to the front door of the school building which read 'There's a bomb inside'.

The panic she had hoped to create duly ensued, the school was rapidly evacuated and Jennifer was able to quietly slip away and do whatever it was she was so desperate to do. Two days later, however, she was arrested by the police, who had presumably nailed her as the person responsible after a quick bit of handwriting analysis, and the game was up. She was subsequently charged with false reporting of explosives, a class six felony apparently, which sounds jolly serious.

It quickly emerged that Jennifer had previous when it came to not exactly putting the kids first, having been charged in 2009 with two counts of misdemeanour child abuse, and in 2010 with travelling with an unrestrained child in a car, and Escuela de Guadallupe officials suddenly had to explain what the hell they had been playing at employing her in the first place. 'The safety and well-being of our kids is our top priority and we are confident that we are providing this type of environment right now,' spluttered a spokesman unconvincingly. 'We are not able to get into the particulars of personnel matters. At this point the matter is now in the hands of the Denver police and the Denver DA's office.'

Jennifer got a four-year suspended sentence and 180 days house arrest for her ill-advised actions – as well as the sack obviously – but the final twist in the tale was her part-time employment status. Her contract with the school was to teach just *one* day a week.

THE DANGERS OF DECENT EXPOSURE

READING, 2011

The dawn of the digital age has, on balance, proved something of a mixed blessing for the teaching profession. The possibilities provided by information technology have undoubtedly pushed the educational envelope to new levels, but on the flip side teachers do now have to spend an inordinate amount of their time confiscating iPads, wrestling with the evil that is the Excel spreadsheet and explaining to outraged parents that those indelicate pictures of them *in flagrante* with the head teacher are merely the result of disgruntled pupils messing about with Photoshop.

The electronic revolution has also brought into sharp focus the thorny issue of digital privacy and teachers today must be ever vigilant to ensure they do not break the avalanche of guidelines concerning pupil safety. It's a minefield out there folks, make no mistake.

An ultimately innocent victim of the tectonic shift in education was a German teacher by the name of Christopher Hammond, who unexpectedly found himself unemployed after 11 years teaching at the Abbey School in Reading, after taking a group of kids on a week-long trip to the land of bratwurst, *Johann Sebastian Bach* and Boris Becker in 2011.

Christopher did not lose a single student, none of his group overindulged in the local schnapps and he didn't even submit a slightly suspicious expenses claim at the end of the trip. No, Christopher's crime was to take some 870 photographs documenting the trip on his own camera. The scoundrel.

The problem was that he was meant to do his Annie Leibovitz impression with a school-owned device, or at least use a school memory card to store the images, but being something of a keen amateur snapper, he took his own Nikon. The school was incandescent and accused him of 'flouting guidelines' and 'failing to safeguard pupils' personal data'. The secretary was ordered to hastily arrange his marching orders and Christopher was shown the door.

At this point you would not be overly cynical to politely enquire of the nature of the photographs, but here's the rub, even the school conceded from the outset of the legal proceedings that ensued that there was absolutely nothing untoward or troubling about the images whatsoever. Unless you find pictures of German men in Lederhosen disturbing. Which let's face it, most right-thinking people do.

The tribunal that resulted eventually ruled that Christopher had been unfairly dismissed but it was probably scant consolation after being put through the legal wringer. He did at least fare slightly better than the teacher who took his class on an ill-advised cultural trip to North Korea, whipped out his camera and found himself spending five years in solitary confinement.

SACRILEGE IN SAN BENITO

CALIFORNIA, USA, 2012

America tends to take religion jolly seriously. After all, the US boasts the largest number of Christians on the planet, with an estimated 247 million worshippers. By any measure that is an awful lot of devotees of Jesus, and suffice to say our transatlantic cousins are not big fans of blasphemy.

Teachers who dip their toes into the perilous waters of religion in the classroom, therefore, do so very much at their own risk, but rather than go for a gentle paddle our next educator, Imelda Paredes, dived in headlong with two-and-half somersaults in the pike position and, as result of her heretical splash, found herself hung out to dry.

The incident occurred at the San Benito's Veterans High School in California during a Spanish class for a group of 14- and 15-year-olds. Normality prevailed at the start of Imelda's class, but things went a bit turbo when she suddenly launched into a 12-minute tirade, in which she inexplicably made a series of increasingly bizarre and utterly blasphemous claims.

She kicked off with a real attention grabber, insisting that Jesus had got Mary Magdalene pregnant before he was crucified. Imelda, by now speaking in Spanish, said that the son of God and Ms Magdalene had first met when she was 12, and in the years that followed they became quite an item and were frequently spotted together at parties.

There was much, much more. Our erratic educator

claimed she was in fact Magdalene reincarnated and that when she went to heaven she and Jesus would tie the knot and she would have his child. It was unclear whether this would be an immaculate conception or not.

And there was yet more. Imelda then got a bit tangential and revealed that an army despatched by God was poised to destroy the Earth on 21 December 2012, but that her students need not worry because Jesus had created another planet, a Utopia replete with waterfalls, where everybody was perpetually 25 years old and money did not exist. Christmas, however, survived the cut although it was not spelled out how people could afford presents if they didn't have any cash. There was also something about volcanoes and a UFO piloted by the Virgin Mary but you've probably got the picture by now.

We know all this because Imelda's meltdown was inevitably caught on the phone camera of one of her students and she was removed from the classroom in mid-flow after an alarmed pupil had slipped out to get help. She was suspended from duties for the remainder of the academic year and a supply teacher whose religious views were rather more orthodox was hastily parachuted in.

The local San Benito schools superintendent subsequently claimed that Imelda's heretical behaviour was a result of a bad reaction to the prescription drugs she was taking on doctor's orders. The mind-altering potential of powerful pharmaceuticals is well documented. It would, of course, be remiss to suggest the same could be said of religion.

CASHING IN ON CAMERA
CALIFORNIA, USA, 2012

It was Shakespeare's portly character of Falstaff who sagely observed in *Henry IV, Part I* that 'nothing confutes me but eyes, and nobody sees'. He was musing on the vagaries of crime, and prior to stabbing the corpse of the slain Hotspur and claiming the credit for his demise, reasoned that if no one actually witnessed his deceit, he was assured of getting away with it. Or to put it another way, without evidence, whatever the crime, you ain't doing the time.

Proof was definitely the problem for the students at Linden High School in California in 2012 after a spate of thefts from their school bags. Cash had been going missing on a frustratingly regular basis as they took sports classes and one of the kids, a young lady by the name of Justine Betti, decided enough was enough and decided to skip gym, hold her own stakeout in the changing rooms and catch the callous culprit in the act. Nancy Drew would have been proud.

Justine hid herself in a locker and was amazed to see one of Linden's very own teachers rifling through the unattended bags and helping themselves to any cash they could lay their thieving hands on. Justine knew teachers didn't earn a king's ransom but she had never suspected their salaries were that skinny – let alone their morals.

The problem was that none of her peers believed her tale of scholastic skullduggery. Justine, though, was nothing if not persistent and she subsequently returned to her hidey-hole, but this time she was armed with her mobile, and when our greedy member of staff returned to help themselves to some more of the kids' lunch money, she caught them red-handed on camera.

'I didn't want to believe that she would do something like that because she was so nice, but then she did it,' Justine said. 'It was really scary. Something needed to be done. That's not okay. I was like, "Oh my gosh. I can't believe I just got this on video".'

After sharing her evidence with her classmates and singularly failing to resist the temptation to tell them she had told them so, Justine marched purposefully to the principal's office with her shocking revelation. The principal rather furtively mumbled something about an investigation but told her to delete the incriminating video of the teacher, only to be told by Justine that she'd already shared it with the rest of her class and her parents and it was too late for an establishment cover-up to try and salvage the school's reputation.

The anonymous kleptomaniac was put on suspension, pending further enquiries by the local sheriff's department. She may or may not have muttered, 'I would have got away with it if it hadn't been for that pesky kid,' as she cleared her desk.

IN THE FIRING LINE
VIRGINIA, USA, 2012

It's one of the immutable laws of education that some subjects are just that little bit sexier than others. Coquettish courses, such as media studies and sociology, for example, are the attractive new kids on the block, while classes like religious studies and applied statistics are seen as more dowdy and frequently find themselves the wallflowers at the school disco.

156

The time-honoured art of welding is sadly in the latter category. It's true that some vocationally minded students do beat a conscious path to the metalwork classroom, but the allure of the acetylene torch is not for all, and the pretty young things on the syllabus like Mandarin and politics maintain a self-satisfied disdain for arc cutting and edge joints.

American teacher, Manuael Dillow, was acutely aware that the members of his welding class in Virginia were not exactly gripped by the subject. In fact they were distinctly underwhelmed by ferrous metals and fillet welds and Manuael was evidently desperate to liven up his classroom a bit. For reasons we shall never fully understand, he decided to shoot his students.

It would, of course, not be a tale for comic retelling had he actually gunned down his class. As we shall learn, Manuael proved to be a bit of a nutter, but he wasn't a certified psychopath and he was mercifully not responsible for a bloodbath. Instead he lined up 12 of his young charges against a wall, whipped out a pistol from inside his belt and fired ten blank rounds at his startled students before they'd even had chance to start work on their tee joints.

It didn't take long for the police to arrive, armed to the teeth, and after apprehending Manuael, he was charged with 12 felony counts of brandishing a firearm – one for each of the dozen terrified youngsters – and inciting fear in the students, which was rather understating the emotion he had elicited at gunpoint from his class. Each felony charge carried a maximum sentence of five years in prison and, after consulting a colleague who taught maths, Manuael realised to his considerable chagrin he was facing 60 years behind bars. Considering he was 60 at the time of the incident it wasn't looking good for his impending retirement.

It later transpired he had 'borrowed' the offending handgun from a fellow educator who taught criminal justice at the same school and used the pistol as a visual aid in his classes. Manuael had decided to follow suit, but it was obviously not the best idea he'd ever had, ranking alongside his decision to become a metalwork teacher in the first place.

Remarkably some of the parents whose kids had (literally) been in the firing line publicly stood by our trigger-happy welder, but the court was unmoved by their support, and handed Manuael a five-year suspended sentence for his ill-judged ballistic outburst.

STUDENTS
IN THE DOG HOUSE
FLORIDA, USA, 2012

A career in education is not always a teacher's first job. Many have dabbled in other professions before finding their true calling as a sculptor of young minds, and our classrooms are replete with repentant lawyers, rehabilitated police personnel as well as former bank manager and bus drivers, butchers and bakers. Not so much the candlestick makers these days, what with the advent of electricity, but the point is that numerous teachers have earned a crust elsewhere before joining the academic ranks.

Laurie Bailey-Cutkomp used to work in a vet's office over in the USA before she decided to change career, hit the books and qualify as a science teacher. She subsequently landed a job at Zephyrhills High School in Florida but, it seems, struggled to entirely leave her old life behind.

The problem, as ever, was discipline. Tardiness and the consumption of fizzy drinks in class were Laurie's particular *bêtes noires*, but rather than go down the traditional route of detention or a visit to the principal's office, she devised a bizarre punishment to keep the kids in line. Laurie made them wear the 'cone of shame': a wraparound plastic collar worn around the neck that obscured the head. Sound familiar? That's because it was exactly the same as the plastic cones favoured by vets to prevent dogs and cats interfering with their stitches after surgery.

Cue the ubiquitous influence of social media as pictures of

Laurie's unusual disciplinary regime appeared on Facebook and all hell inevitably broke loose. 'She has shown extremely poor judgement,' fumed the local schools superintendent, who called for her to be sacked immediately. 'I am stunned you would put dog collars on students for any reason.'

Quite, although to be fair Laurie's antics rather split opinion at the school. 'I was disgusted, very disgusted,' one parent said after being informed what had been going on. 'That's a human, not an animal. You're not spaying or neutering that person.' Some of the pupils, however, were prepared to see the funny side of things. 'All the parents were commenting on it saying she should get fired but she just did it as a joke and said she was going to punish us by doing it,' said one. 'But she asked us first and we were all laughing and joking around.'

Laurie herself claimed she drew inspiration for her surreal punishment after showing her class the animated Pixar film *Up,* in which a dog is forced to wear the 'cone of shame' for being disobedient, but we know it really came from seeing a succession of real-life dogs trooping in and out of the vet's office reluctantly sporting plastic hoods.

159

Remarkably she dodged the bullet of unemployment. It took the authorities four months to decide what to do with Laurie but they eventually settled on moving her to a different school rather than end her teaching career. 'She is a certified science teacher and we've had a very difficult time finding them,' said principal Kim Anderson, her new boss at Pasco Middle School. 'I am very excited that she is going to have this new opportunity. She starts on Monday and she's excited.'

Whether her new pupils shared that sense of excitement is debatable, given her reputation, but every single pupil was on time for their first lesson and there wasn't a solitary can of cola in sight.

THE SYDNEY CENTURION
AUSTRALIA, 2012

The retirement age for teachers in the UK currently stands at 65. If you joined the profession before 2007 you can get your hands on your pension when you turn 60, while some lucky mortals bid farewell to the classroom for the last time even earlier, but the general rule is that when weary educators hit their sixth decade, they can finally remove their mortar boards, hang up their gowns and stop pretending to actually like children.

It is a rare breed indeed who do not look forward to retirement with a gleeful sense of anticipation, but there are always exceptions to the educational rule, and in 2012 an Australian by the name of Father Geoffrey Schneider proved age had certainly not withered him one iota when he entered into the *Guinness World Records* as the oldest, active, full-time teacher on the planet.

Father Schneider celebrated his one-hundredth birthday in December 2012, but it was in October that year that the then 99-year-old Catholic priest and staff member at the St Aloysius' College in the suburbs of Sydney was officially anointed as teaching's most aged practitioner, a remarkable feat of endurance that rather made the rest of the profession look like fly-by-night quitters.

After scholastic stints at schools in his hometown of Melbourne and then Perth, Father Schneider arrived at St Aloysius in 1965 and was still strutting his stuff in the classroom 47 years later to earn his unchallenged place in the academic record books.

Affectionately nicknamed 'Father Schnitzel' by the thousands upon thousands of students who had sat in his class over the decades, the Father ascribed his incredible longevity to his refusal to lose his patience with his students and a morbid fear of retirement. 'You must have a mountain of patience,' he said. 'If things are going wrong, don't start shouting. Just proceed quietly and things will settle down eventually. Their books will eventually open. Retirement? So I can read the paper every morning and then forget what's in it? That's what a retired friend told me happens to him. At 3p.m. there's afternoon tea and if you don't turn up in the first minute they come knock on your door and say, "It's tea time now". It just doesn't appeal to me. I just feel I can be more useful here.'

It took *Guinness World Records* months of characteristically painstaking research to verify the Father's claim and when they were finally satisfied there was no one older than him in the business, they sent their man Down Under, Chris Sheedy, to present him with official confirmation of the record. By a strange twist of fate, Chris just happened to be one of 'Father Schnitzel's' former pupils.

'When your teacher is almost 80 years old, as Father was when I attended St Aloysius' College [in the 1980s], you can't help but absorb all they say,' Chris said at the ceremony. 'To hand Father the certificate was a great honour. He is a man who has touched the lives of tens of thousands of students, always in a positive and supportive way. He has been a part of the life of many of our country's leading sports stars, musical talents, politicians, actors, authors, artists, medical professionals and business people and one very thankful GWR rep.' Bless.

At the time of going to press the redoubtable Father Schneider was still going strong, his only complaint that pupils these days seemed to be getting even younger and younger.

CAUGHT SHORT AT CASTLE VALE

BIRMINGHAM, 2012

Every recently appointed head teacher likes to make their mark on their new school. The need to show staff, parents and pupils alike that there's a new sheriff in town is in their DNA, and although the first step is invariably a shiny new name plate on the door to their office, a deluge of decrees and diktats inevitably follow to prove to people that they're really, you know, getting to grips with the job.

That burning desire to stamp their authority on proceedings can, however, frequently lead to friction, and it was certainly fractious in the extreme at the Castle Vale Performing Arts College in Birmingham, when the new *grand fromage*, Charlotte Blencowe, pitched up in 2012 and almost overnight alienated the entire school community. Charlotte may have had an ambitious grand plan for the college, but during her brief stint at Castle Vale she would have comfortably lost a popularity contest with the Khmer Rouge, Inland Revenue or even Jeffrey Archer.

Her first major edict from on high was the implementation of that old chestnut, a strict new dress code. She was far from the first head to make such a move, but when 40 students were sent home on the first day of term for wearing the wrong shoes, a group of angry parents staged a protest outside the school, police were called and some of the teachers were pelted with eggs.

Not the best start then, but things were to go from bad to

worse. Charlotte decided the student body at Castle Vale really needed to focus in their lessons and to facilitate this she introduced two bizarre new rules which rather annoyed parents and pupils.

The first was the banning of all talking in classrooms, replacing verbal communication with a series of hand signals. Fingers pointed to the eyes and then towards the board meant the student could not see properly. Hands clasped together in the air translated as I need a need new book or paper, while raising one finger equated to a request for a pencil or pen.

Charlotte's second and even more controversial innovation was the introduction of 'tinkle passes', a piece of paper that allowed pupils to go to the toilet. Emblazoned with the words 'I am missing a super learning opportunity because I need a tinkle', the passes were handed out on Monday morning – one per student – and if they had not been redeemed, had to be returned on Friday afternoon. That's right, pupils were permitted only one comfort break every five days and there were no rollovers.

Guess what? There was uproar, obviously. 'It's ridiculous because what happens if the child needs to use the toilet during class more than once a week,' seethed one parent. 'What are they supposed to do, wet themselves?'

The rudimentary experiment in classroom sign language proved no more popular. 'It's a secondary school but they're treating it more like a nursery with all these hand signals and tinkle cards.

'My kids are saying to me, "Mum, we're not at school, we're at a prison". They're not allowed to talk in class at all and must do everything by these bizarre hand signals.'

The new head also wanted to make it mandatory for 15-year-old English students to read *How to Lose Friends & Alienate People*, but gave up because the English department couldn't stop laughing.

'We put her name forward to the board of governors

because we believed she was the right candidate,' said a spokesman for the Academies Enterprise Trust as the furore raged. 'The first week in a new school is always challenging. We are confident we will secure a stronger and better future for Castle Vale Performing Arts College. She is here to stay.'

Except that she wasn't. Just three months after pitching up at the school, Charlotte was gone, presumably taking her controversial tinkle passes with her. Rumours that parents gave her a leaving card with the message 'I am missing a super employment opportunity because I need my head examining' written inside are unfounded.

INSTITUTIONALISED INSOMNIA IN RUSSIA

RUSSIA, 2012

Despite the sage advice of experienced educators that it is prudent to report for exams alert and fully refreshed, it is far from unusual for bleary-eyed students to sit down to tackle their end-of-year papers having pulled an all-nighter in a desperate bid to cram in as much last-gasp, fevered revision as the wee hours will allow.

Fuelled by an inexhaustible supply of coffee, energy drinks and a growing sense of panic, pupils frequently eschew sleep as they frantically try to memorise the periodic table, or fix in their minds at three o'clock in the morning whether it was Hamlet or Macbeth whose night-time apparitions involved a bloody knife.

Yes, revision can play havoc with sleep patterns but in this next strange tale it was the exam itself rather than the preparations for it that left a group of utterly exhausted students in urgent need of forty winks.

We head to Russia and the Kazan State University where a group of 15 nuclear physics undergraduates had gathered in 2012 for their final exams. They reported for duty at ten o'clock in the morning but remarkably they were not allowed to leave the examination room until nine the following morning. That's a 23-hour stretch in anyone's money.

The villain of this particular piece was lecturer Landysh Zaripova, who was in charge of the oral exams but rather lost track of time. And, according to the students, her grip on sobriety. Zaripova, they alleged, was three sheets to the wind, refused to let any of them go to the toilet or eat for the entire duration and spent the 23 hours haranguing them.

'Towards the end, everyone was just sitting there, totally exhausted,' complained one student after the ordeal. 'The lecturer would go into another room, drink, come back and start telling us about her business interests. She stank of alcohol.'

Zaripova hit back, however, insisting that the exam had lasted so long simply because it had been a protracted process completing all the oral assessments and she vehemently denied having one too many vodkas. 'The group was big – 15 people, and the subject difficult,' she said. 'It's hard to pass in nuclear physics. I was not drunk. Do you think I am an idiot? I was sober. The students just decided to get revenge on me because they couldn't pass the exam.'

The students lodged a formal complaint against Zaripova, calling for her to be sacked, but the head of the University's Physics Department was forced to admit that even if the allegations had been proven, he would have been powerless to act as he she had a five-year, 'unbreakable' contract and was effectively untouchable.

A menacing Russian authority figure who is seemingly impossible to get rid of? Remind you of anyone?

CLIVE'S KIDNAP CAPER

CANTERBURY, 2012

Fuelling a child's imagination is at the very heart of education. Any stimuli which get those juvenile synapses firing is to be commended, and these days schools are perpetually in search of exciting ways to bring their subjects to life. It's the iPad generation for you – books alone are just so twentieth century. Not this one obviously, it really should go without saying.

The headmaster of Wincheap Primary in Canterbury certainly subscribed to that school of thought in 2012 when he was contemplating creative writing lessons for nine- and ten-year-olds. Clive Close, for that was his name, wanted to give the lessons a bit more va-va voom, and when he realised the school couldn't quite stretch to sending the kids for a two-week sojourn in the Latin Quarter of Paris, he settled on a cheaper alternative to get the pupils' creative juices flowing.

Canny Clive decided to stage a fake kidnap outside the school and get the kids to write eyewitness accounts of what they'd seen. He stepped into the lead role of kidnapper, donning a white jump suit and red wig, while the school's site manager gave a poignant portrayal of the kidnappee as Clive waved around a tap from a sink in lieu of a pistol and deposited his 'victim' into the boot of his Audi. A top theatrical effort fellas!

The only problem was that no one had told witnesses that

this was all a set-up and it was not long before the leading bastion of national morality, also known as the *Daily Mail*, was decrying Clive's stunt.

'Stunned nine and ten-year-olds watched from their classroom window as, in a few terrifying seconds, he abducted the school caretaker, bundled him into a car and screeched off into the distance,' the newspaper fumed. 'For a moment it looked as if a major crime had been committed before the eyes of dozens of little innocents. It also drew criticism from some parents after it emerged that the head teacher had not warned police he was going to be waving a pretend firearm around.'

The report proceeded to give voice to a cacophony of alleged parent disapproval. 'I am of the opinion – as are several other parents – that primary school children should not be scared stiff in class,' one unnamed parent was quoted as saying while another mused, 'You can imagine that if this took place at an inner-city primary the head teacher could well have been shot dead by armed police.'

Clive, however, was unrepentant, stood firmly by his unusual lesson format and insisted he had not received a single complaint. Not even from the caretaker. 'If you sit kids in classrooms and try and teach them things they can't connect with, and it's dry and unexciting, you will lose them,' he said. 'Particularly the kids in this school. The papers have manipulated this to produce a story. The saying "never let the truth get in the way of a good story" has never been more apt.'

Take that, *Daily Mail*. More parents joined the debate but this time they were all fully signed-up members of Team Clive. 'We all think he's fabulous and since he became head the school has smashed its targets for literacy', one mother told the Kent Online website. 'My ten-year-old daughter Maisie was in the lesson when the fake kidnap was staged and she could not believe how ridiculous some of the reporting about it had been.' One father wrote to the school: 'Everything I hear and observe about yours, and the school's, approach and the astonishing turnaround that you've achieved at Wincheap since you started, gives me every confidence in the education my daughter is receiving.'

Clive's aforementioned Audi made another appearance in the news in 2015 but this time it was unfortunately because he was pulled over by the police whilst over the limit behind the wheel. This time it sadly wasn't a hoax and proved that engaging in a war of words with the *Daily Mail* is enough to turn anyone to drink.

THE GREAT POSSUM MASSACRE

NEW ZEALAND, 2012

Money may indeed make the world go round but it's also frightfully handy for cash-strapped schools that need to buy things. In theory the local authority stumps up the readies for the absolute essentials – you know, books, pens, heating and stuff like that – but should a school wish to purchase something deemed by the bean counters as extravagant and extracurricular, a new computer perhaps, they're usually on their own.

Step forwards the ubiquitous school fundraiser, the brazen attempt to part parents from their hard-earned cash. There are a myriad ways to get Mr and Mrs Griffiths to hand over that tenner, and while the simple, halcyon days of the car boot sale are largely a distant memory, they have been superseded by such modern upstarts as the slave auction, the sponsored bungee jump and selling the hacking talents of 5B to the highest bidder.

Over in New Zealand, however, they take a distinctly more macabre approach to the swelling of the scholastic coffers, and you needed a strong stomach indeed in 2012, when the Uruti School in Taranaki launched an annual fundraiser, which had a sickening emphasis on harnessing the local natural resources.

More specifically, the pupils' parents went out and shot as many possums as they could point their shotguns at. The corpses were brought home and the kids were encouraged to pose and dress the bodies before rigor mortis set in and the school had itself a bizarre, post mortem, possum fancy dress competition. There were dead possums in bikinis, wedding dresses and babygrows complete with bibs. One of the deceased marsupials was shaved and posed to look like a boxer, while another rocked the Vincent van Gogh look. Unfortunately for our brush-tailed possums, while they are a protected species across the sea in Australia, they are considered a pest in New Zealand, hence the extermination at Uruti.

There was still something of brouhaha in the wake of the school's slaughter, and opinion was split on whether the possum massacre and subsequent 'best dressed' show was a good or a bad thing. 'There was an amazing crowd and it was lots of fun,' said the school principal Pauline Sutton. 'Animals aren't the only species who are dressed up after they die. We do it to humans too. My chairperson has received lots of phone calls from hunters and the local community all saying how great they thought the day was. We work with the Department of Conservation and the Kiwi Trust. I think we are very understanding of the wild life around us.'

Pauline and her armed supporters certainly understood *where* to find the poor possums. Her argument, however, failed to win over the Society for the Prevention of Cruelty to Animals. 'Our focus is on teaching children respect and empathy for animals and they didn't do that,' a spokeswoman said. 'Animals deserve respect even after death. Children are impressionable and this isn't teaching them to respect animals. It leads on to relationships with people, if they respect animals it leads to humans, there's a link there.'

Many locals weren't impressed either. 'Teaching kids that killing then dressing up the dead bodies of animals as a form of entertainment is one of the sickest things I've seen,' posted one resident on the *Taranaki Daily News* website.

OK, so back to the whole fundraising theme. The ghoulish

shenanigans at Uruti raised a grand total of £4,000 but there was an added financial bonus as a result of the event: the school saved a further £500 from the biology department budget as it no longer needed to spend money on deliveries of rats for dissection classes.

MINNIE'S MOTORING MADNESS

SOUTH AFRICA, 2012

As every teacher is acutely aware, taking children 'off site' is a logistical nightmare in the modern era of education. The number of forms that must be completed in triplicate before students can leave the school premises generates a paper mountain to dwarf Kilimanjaro, while the risk assessment required rivals even that which would be undertaken by the CIA ahead of an American Presidential motorcade along the less salubrious streets of downtown Baghdad.

Well, that's at least how it works here in the UK these days, but other countries seem to have a distressingly more *laissez faire* attitude to letting their pupils explore beyond the playground and, more pertinently, how the little darlings get from A to B.

South African nursery school teacher Melanie Minnie alarmingly illustrated the point in 2012 when she decided to treat a group of four- to six-year-olds with a little trip to the local shopping mall in Pretoria to grab a burger. Melanie had 19 kids to transport but sadly the school minibus was at the garage and she just couldn't face frogmarching the group all the way on foot.

There was only one solution – Mel decided to squeeze her class into her Renault Clio. As any *Top Gear* aficionado will know, a Clio is far from the most capacious motor available on the market, but perhaps she'd been a junior sardines champion and thus was determined to successfully cram the tots into the vehicle. Six were stuffed unceremoniously into the boot, three awkwardly shared the passenger seat, while the remaining ten occupied the back seats. The group then set off for their quarter pounders and cheese.

She would have got away with it as well if hadn't been for the meddling kids and a concerned onlooker who spotted Mel unloading her cramped charges at the aforementioned shopping mall. A frantic call to the local constabulary followed and the police were despatched to investigate.

To make matters worse, a local photographer by the name of Nico van Heerden had spotted the bizarre school trip, and taken an incriminating picture of Mel's ridiculously overloaded motor. 'They were excited at first,' he told local reporters, 'but after a while they started to get worried and cried.' At least those who could actually breathe did.

The long arm of the law quickly caught up with our foolish nursery school teacher and pointed out that unless she had 19 seat belts and a Clio that did a passable impression of the Tardis, she was in hot water. She was fined 1,500 rand (around £75) and told not to be so … stupid again. 'I was startled to get pulled over,' Mel said. 'It was the first time we went on an outing. And the last time.'

Luckily all the children emerged from the ordeal unscathed. It was, after all, a car crèche waiting to happen.

SERPENT AT HIGH SCOOL
KENTUCKY, USA, 2012

Ever since Adam and Eve fell spectacularly foul of the evil machinations of the serpent in the Garden of Eden, mankind has had a rather ambivalent attitude to snakes. Some people adore the writhing vertebrates and keep them as pets, but it's fair to say that most prefer to give them a distinctly wide berth and unless you find yourself in the unlikely situation of appearing on *I'm a Celebrity ... Get Me Out of Here!*, the chances are you need never make their slippery acquaintance.

Which is probably exactly what Hopkinsville High School teacher Wanda Jones misguidedly believed when she was sitting in her office in 2006, blissfully minding her own business. Kentucky is not exactly awash with snakes and the last thing Wanda probably expected was to be confronted with a serpent completely out of the blue.

What she didn't know was that a mother of one of the students had brought a snake into school for a science class and handed it over to vice principal Cynthia Dougherty, who suddenly appeared in the doorway clutching the hissing reptile. Wanda looked up and, according to the subsequent court papers, 'jumped out of her seat and started screaming and ran into the concrete wall,' behind her. The snake lifted its head and put its tongue out and she continued 'screaming and screaming and screaming while Dougherty just stood there.'

Wanda claimed she suffered injuries to her knees and heart as a result of the incident as well as post-traumatic stress syndrome, and after years of legal wrangling, the case finally got to court in 2012 on appeal after Cynthia had initially been exonerated of 'intentionally and maliciously carrying a large snake' into Wanda's office.

'Dougherty stated that she did not enter the office but remained in the doorway,' the court heard. 'Dougherty admitted that Wanda seemed surprised when she looked up and saw the snake. However, Dougherty did not say that Wanda screamed or that she jumped from her chair and ran into the wall. Furthermore, Dougherty stated that she was only in the doorway to Wanda's office for approximately ten seconds and that the snake was curled up in her arms and not moving.'

Dougherty also argued that she 'did not specifically intend to kill or cause serious physical injury,' but the pivotal legal argument was the assertion that you couldn't really blame Cynthia because Wanda had neglected to tell her she was terrified of snakes. It was a defence on a par with shooting someone and then justifying it because the victim hadn't previously articulated their fear of bullets, but incredibly the appeal court bought it and Dougherty was acquitted of all charges.

Mercifully the case did not open the floodgates for other teachers to terrify colleagues in the staff room with the more menacing members of the animal kingdom. Dougherty tried to mend bridges with Wanda after all the unpleasantness but her conciliatory gift of the DVD of *Snakes on a Plane* was at best ill judged. (But I might have made that up.)

THE COMPENSATION CULTURE
SOMERSET, 2013

Schools can be hazardous to a teacher's health. Granted a day trip to Chernobyl, or an afternoon stroll around the minefields of Iraq, are probably more dangerous but potential perils lurk in even the humblest of educational establishments. Teachers venture on a daily basis where angels fear to tread.

The risks are myriad. The reams of paper that educators confront are a nasty paper cut just waiting to happen, the swill that frequently passes for coffee in the staff room can strip paint, while our brave educators takes their lives into their own hands when they reluctantly let the class loose on the Bunsen burners.

Some mishaps and injuries sustained by teachers are, however, of the more surreal nature and, to paraphrase a line from a TV ad for one of those personal injury law firms, even if there's no blame there's still a claim.

Our first example of spurious litigation after an accident at work comes from 2012 when a teacher was strolling through the dining hall at Backwell School in Somerset. The teacher spotted a piece of discarded ham lying on the floor and, in an effort to sidestep the abandoned pork product, she inadvertently trod on 'something gooey' and took a bit of a tumble. InjuryLawyers4U were all over it like a rash, and although Somerset County Council quite reasonably argued that finding 'something gooey' on the floor of the school eatery was hardly the height of negligence, they were nonetheless ordered to cough up £17,000 in compensation.

It was a similar story in Yorkshire when Kirklees Council found themselves £20,000 poorer when one of their teaching staff took them to court after they were bitten by a flea in the workplace. The authorities argued the flea wasn't a council employee, but after consulting with lawyers, got their chequebook out to save a few additional quid. 'The case was settled out of court following legal advice and the claimant received compensation of around £5,000,' a spokesman explained. 'The remainder was spent on the necessary legal fees. Other medical conditions meant the bite became infected, leading to swelling and ulceration and up to two years of pain. This was an unusual situation.' You can say that again.

In 2008 it was Essex County Council's turn to reluctantly raid their educational coffers, when one of their teachers slipped on a sachet of tomato ketchup *en route* to the staff room and got litigious, the council eventually shelling out £90,000 in damages, £120,000 in legal fees and £20,000 in costs. In Hounslow a teacher was once awarded £56,000 for facial injuries after being hit in the face with a set of maracas. To this day the school maintains it has absolutely no idea who booked the mariachi band.

In Rochdale, a teacher who strained their back lifting a table boosted their bank balance to the tune of £10,663. Exactly how the courts decide on these settlement figures remains a mystery, but the strong suspicion must be that they simply pull the numbers out of a bag.

One of the longest-running and easily most ridiculous compensation cases saw South Gloucestershire Council fight an eight-year legal battle with an employee after he had been taking a sports lesson and, horror of horrors, got his foot stuck in a football net. And, if you're of a squeamish disposition don't read on – he fell over. He wanted £30,000 for his injuries, not least to his pride, and although the council maintained it was not unreasonable to find football nets on a football pitch, the court ordered them to pay almost £83,000. To add insult to, ahem, injury, only £619.50 went to our vertically challenged educator, the rest was swallowed up by legal costs.

So if you've ever mused how your taxes are invested in terms of schools spending, you have your answer.

MARIA'S JUVENILE AVERSION

OHIO, USA, 2013

You don't, strictly, have to like children to become a teacher. An affection for the younger members of society definitely helps, though, if you intend to spend six or more hours a day, five days a week, in close proximity to them, but nowhere on the application form does it explicitly state that would-be educators have to be particularly fond of the next generation.

Suffering from an active and acute physical aversion to children, however, is an altogether different story. Pedophobes really have no business in a classroom and should immediately seek alternative employment as librarians. Modern school children wouldn't be seen dead in a library.

Pity then, American teacher, Maria Waltherr-Willard, a self-confessed pedophobia sufferer, who successfully battled her condition for more than two decades to pursue a career in education, only to suddenly find herself confronted with her worse fears.

Maria began working for the Mariemont school district in Ohio in the late 1970s but in the 1990s began to develop pedophobia. She made no secret of her affliction to her bosses, but insisted that if she only had to educate the high school-age kids, the 14- to 18-year-olds, she'd be OK. It was, she confessed, the younger children who really freaked her out.

For years the arrangement worked just tickety-boo as she taught French and Spanish to successive classes of reassuringly large teenagers. Disaster struck, however, in 2010 when the district's French courses all went online and education bosses asked Maria to *habla Español* face-to-face with a group of 12-year-olds in one of their middle schools. They were way too childlike for her liking but, despite her protestations, they refused to find Maria a group of mini adults to educate, and in 2013 the lawyers were inevitably called in to scavenge on the bones of the dispute.

'The suit claims the discrimination is based on her age and her disability, a rare phobia called pedophobia, which in this context means an extreme fear or anxiety around young children,' reported *USA Today*. 'Waltherr-Willard's lawsuit claims she has suffered from the condition since the 1990s and that Mariemont had made assurances to her and her lawyer that she would not have to teach young children.

'Documents filed in the case by her medical doctor, psychiatrists and psychologists note that she experiences stress, anxiety, chest pains, vomiting, nightmares and higher than healthy blood pressure when she's around young children.'

The wheels of justice turned slowly and it was not until 2015 that Maria learned she'd been unsuccessful in proving disability discrimination, the Sixth US Circuit Court of Appeals in Cincinnati dismissing the case on the grounds the school had never actually signed anything agreeing that she wouldn't be required to teach the little 'uns. Maria was forced to take early retirement to extricate herself from her unbearable situation, but it was sadly not before the American media had enjoyed much mirth at her expense, with mocking tales of the teacher who was scared of school children and so forth.

Imagine what kind of film *The Sound of Music* would have been if another famous Maria, namely the future Mrs von Trapp, had also suffered from pedophobia. The kids would never have got past 'Doe, a deer, a female deer …' before she was out of the door.

A PREMATURE
CLASSROOM ARRIVAL

LONDON, 2013

The peel of the morning bell signalling the beginning of another day at the mad house can have varying effects on teachers. For the more bright-eyed among the educational ranks, it signifies new possibilities and new adventures, while for those with a few more miles on the clock, it merely confirms there are six-and-a-half hours until the blessed relief of home time.

For Diane Krish-Veeramany however, the ring of the bell one morning at her primary school in Hainult, north-east London, had an altogether more dramatic impact, suddenly sending the unsuspecting teacher into labour a month early – and just one day before she was scheduled to sign off on maternity leave.

Diane reported for duty at Manford Primary School as usual, happily stroking her bump, but half an hour before the day was due to start she began to feel peculiar. She soldiered on, but as she waited in the classroom for the kids to troop in, her contractions kicked in and baby was well and truly *en route*.

There was no time for an ambulance. There wasn't even time to get to the staff room. There was no time to call the school nurse because it wasn't the 1950s and the school didn't have one, and so Diane was whisked into an empty classroom and three teaching assistants were pressed into emergency service as midwives to help deliver the baby, the trio taking instructions over the phone from paramedics. Much huffing and puffing and wailing and screaming inevitably ensued, but it wasn't long before little Jonah arrived, tipping the scales at a healthy 9lb (4.1kg).

'Everyone who has had a baby knows you try and plan these things in your head but everything happened so quickly,' Diane told the *Daily Mail*. 'It was nothing like I had imagined. It was so perfect, he's completely fine, I'm completely fine, and I'm grateful because otherwise I would have had it in the back of a car.

'At about 8.20a.m. I texted my husband saying I don't feel right. Then after a staff meeting I spoke to the head and said I felt a bit funny and couldn't stay at school. The head asked if I wanted an ambulance but I refused and said it was nothing serious. I was walking to the other side of the school with my teaching assistant when I felt something.

'The children were about to come in and I said I didn't want the kids seeing me like this because I didn't want to frighten them so we went into a classroom that was not being used. I was adamant I was not going to have a baby on the classroom floor. But 20 minutes after the contractions began and within 40 minutes of telling the head I felt sick, a little bundle of joy arrived. One of the teaching assistants said, "You've got a boy, and he's crying".

'I didn't dream I would have to have my baby in a classroom. I'm still in shock, I really am. I can't believe I had him at school. There was so much hype, all the children were so excited. His dad said he was in such a hurry to get here but he was still late for his first day at school.'

Remarkably, dad Vijaye, managed to successfully navigate the London rush hour traffic and made it to school just in time to witness the birth of his boy and avoid the wrath of Diane. He forgot the towels and hot water, though, and wasn't allowed in the playground at lunchtime.

THE DANGERS OF THE UNDEAD

OREGON, USA, 2013

You can't move for zombies these days. Not literally, obviously, otherwise you'd currently be having your entrails violently ripped from your stomach by a peckish horde of the undead, rather than putting your feet up with a nice cuppa and reading this book. No, the point is that zombies are rather *de rigeur* in modern literature, television and film, and our appetite for terrifying tales of the reanimated is as voracious as is their hunger for human flesh.

It was with this cultural phenomenon in mind that American social studies teacher, Rich Harshberge, decided to inject some, ahem, 'life' into his extracurricular class at Armand Larive Middle School in Oregon, and theme his lessons on surviving a zombie apocalypse.

To be fair to Rich, his innovative class did have a firm educational basis and wasn't just about knives, swords and killing techniques. The students were told to keep a fictional survival journal to help hone their creative writing skills and they were told to pour over *The Zombie Survival Guide: Complete Protection from the Living Dead* to encourage reading. The discussions on the best choice of weapon with which to eviscerate a zombie at close range were merely bloody interludes.

The kids, of course, loved it but the same could sadly not be said of the school or local district officials when a parent complained that little Johnny had been having nightmares.

The moral majority swung into censorious action and the classes were axed.

'The use of zombie-related materials is unfortunate and was not approved in accordance with district curricular policies,' the school said in a statement. 'We extend our regrets to anyone offended by their use. While zombies may be a contemporary topic, the inclusion of zombie-related materials was deemed inappropriate for middle school students and has been replaced with age and content-appropriate materials.'

Rich was not happy and insisted his course was designed to promote reading and writing and not violence. 'It's gotten kids engaged that I wouldn't have gotten engaged before,' he said before heading off for his Grammar For Beginners tutorial.

The decision to cancel the zombie-theme syllabus was nothing if not controversial, dividing opinion down the middle. 'Heaven forbid kids have fun while learning,' said one parent who evidently understood exactly what Rich was trying to do. 'The current reading classes are so boring and the reading materials are outdated. I would love to have any class like this that actually got my kids excited about reading.'

The 'No Zombies' lobby, however, was equally vocal. 'It's inappropriate for any school,' fumed one parent. 'What a stupid thing to even consider. Maybe that teacher plays too many video games.' If she wasn't a fictional cartoon character from *The Simpsons*, Helen Lovejoy would doubtless have chipped in with her famous catchphrase 'Won't somebody please think of the children!'

The school replaced Rich's class with 'Exploratory Reading' lessons but that in turn had to be cancelled when the teacher took the title too literally and some of the kids got scared by the dinosaurs in *The Land That Time Forgot*.

FROZEN RETRIBUTION
CHINA, 2013

If you happen to have had the immeasurable pleasure of driving eastbound on the M25, somewhere between Junctions 16 and 17, you are one of the lucky few. The overwhelming majority of motorists invariably find themselves parked up rather than moving on the tarmac hell that is the London Orbital Motorway, but we digress, the point is that on one particular stretch of the M25 there's an Edwardian brick bridge that bears the legend, in big white letters, 'GIVE PEAS A CHANCE.'

It is reputedly the work of a waggish graffiti artist by the name of Peas, rather than a guerrilla advertising campaign by Birds Eye or the (jolly) Green Giant, but again we digress because what concerns us here is, of course, teachers and how the more sadistic among the profession over in China have indeed given peas a chance – to punish mischievous pupils.

Chinese teachers do not, as you may imagine, force vegetable-averse students to eat the peas, but rather take a bag of frozen *petits pois* and force the miscreant pupil to kneel on the little green fellas. It's a painful punishment, which leaves the kids with deep circular impressions on their skin and aching joints, and would certainly result in legal proceedings should any educator in the USA or Europe be foolish enough to employ the dastardly technique. In 2013, a Chinese student took a picture of the results of the punishment, published them online and was promptly expelled for her whistle-blowing.

Chinese teachers, however, do not have the monopoly on dubious ways of enforcing discipline in the classroom. In 2009, at the Charles Summer Elementary School in New Jersey, the staff were so incensed when a student spilled a jug of water in the cafeteria that they made the offender and, for reasons only known to them, some of his classmates, eat their lunch on the floor off a piece of paper. The punishment lasted for ten days, but the pupils had the last laugh when the inevitable litigation that followed was concluded, and seven of them shared the resulting $500,000 compensation payout.

In the French town of Narbonne, a nursery school employee became so infuriated by the behaviour of one of the children that she tied the offender to a chair to teach 'em a lesson, but landed herself in hot water with the gendarmes, while in the USA, a teacher inexplicably kept her job despite cutting off some of the hair of a seven-year-old pupil because she kept playing with it in class.

The *pièce de resistance* of weird punishments, though, must be an Arizona school's innovative way of dealing with two teenage boys who had become embroiled in a fight. The pugilistic pair were given a stark choice – face suspension or sit in the school playground and hold hands for 15 minutes. The lads chose the latter and for quarter of an hour were mocked mercilessly by their peers as they grasped each other's mitts. To compound their embarrassment the punishment was filmed and quickly went viral.

MONEY FOR NOTHING

FRANCE, 2013

Sadly there is no shortage of examples of teachers being blackmailed by their pupils. Avaricious students have, for example, been known to threaten to expose sensitive personal information about their teachers unless they cough up some cash, while educators who've been stupid enough to have a relationship with one of their pupils have frequently had their bank accounts emptied in a desperate attempt to avoid exposure.

Teachers doing the blackmailing is a less common beast indeed, but it happens, and in 2013 in northern France a greedy educator thought he'd swell his own coffers by demanding money with menaces from the parents of one of the boys in his class.

The lad was, by all accounts, a bit of wrong 'un. His list of misdemeanours was longer than the current Government guidelines on the safe use of scissors in art classes for pupils under the age of 8, and when the boy fired a paper pellet at the teacher's head when his back was turned, dark thoughts of blackmail began to distil. The 'attack' was hardly serious, or even minor for that matter, but the teacher claimed he suffered headaches as a result of the projectile and told the parents he wanted hush money or he would report the incident to the headmaster. With his already extensive CV of crime, the unnamed teacher pointed out, the lad would probably be expelled.

He demanded €10,000 for his silence but the frugal parents bartered him down to €7,500. They agreed to pay by setting up a €300 direct debit into his bank account, and after they had reluctantly acquiesced, he sat back to count his illicit income – perhaps whilst stroking a cat menacingly in the style of a classic Bond villain.

The arrangement lasted for just over six months but disaster struck when the lad was expelled for another transgression. The parents had no reason to continue feathering our greedy teacher's nest and the father went to the headmaster's office to report the financial skulduggery that had been perpetrated by one of his members of staff.

The parents took legal advice while the teacher in question was pulled in by the local gendarmes and politely asked what the hell he thought he was playing at. His defence that the money was for personal tuition fell on deaf ears and the 53-year-old was told in no uncertain terms never to darken a classroom again.

SICK OF SCHOOL
WEST YORKSHIRE, 2013

Teaching is not the profession for everyone. Some lack the prerequisite patience to endure six hours a day besieged by 30 unruly kids, others have a morbid fear of nits, while many potential educators simply want to earn more money. An exception to that last scenario is Michael Steer, a former banker who grew weary of the financial world and decided to trade in his calculator and spreadsheet for a life in the classroom.

'I went into banking from university because I needed a career,' Michael explained. 'I got a job at a major high street bank and rose through the ranks quickly. But the higher up I got, the more I developed a distaste for the working practices and the sales side of it all. It didn't seem a particularly moral business. I didn't see how it was helping anybody and I wanted to do something which I deemed more worthwhile. I looked around, took a step back and realised I wanted a career where I can give something back to society.'

Cue a new job as deputy head and maths teacher at Thornhill Community Academy in West Yorkshire, and were it not for the inescapable fact this book is all about strange tales, we would be able to wrap up Michael's uplifting story right there. The inevitable fly in the ointment is the jolly inconvenient fact that he was physically allergic to his classroom. Yup, our poor educational convert was an anaphylactic accident waiting to happen.

Michael suffered from an allergy to the chemical potassium dichromate, as well as suffering from eczema and dermatitis. Unfortunately, potassium dichromate is found in classroom staples such as red ink, smart boards, plastic chairs, computer screens, glue sticks, folders and marker pens, and one false move resulted in blistering and severe swelling of his hands.

'The three skin conditions essentially combine to create the perfect storm, meaning there's a whole host of things in a classroom I'm allergic to,' he said at the time. 'I can't hold stationery, can't touch the board and can't mark students' work with red pens. Every day I wake up and go to work I'm walking into a giant death trap.'

'When I come into contact with the chemical my hands will balloon or sores will flare up, my knuckles will become stiff and tender to move. It comes and goes, it gets better, and it gets worse. Being in a school environment there's a lot of things I cannot use. If I do come into contact with something my body essentially attacks itself.'

'When doctors first diagnosed it they gave me a whole list of things I was allergic to from aeroplanes to army uniforms, match heads to raw chicken. It's a really bizarre condition that I've had to adapt to. I try to not let it affect me and my job.'

Adapting to his new career meant wearing gloves to avoid an unwelcome flare-up but while many teachers would jokingly say they're allergic to their pupils, Michael really was allergic to school.

And if you're thinking Michael sounds familiar, it's probably because he featured in the acclaimed UK Channel 4 documentary *Educating Yorkshire*. He was the one in the white gloves and the local hospital on speed dial.

A BALLISTIC
MISADVENTURE
WOLVERHAMPTON, 2013

Making lessons more exciting is good. Making lessons more dangerous is bad. It's not exactly a subtle distinction but one that all teachers would do well to heed as they plan how to bring their chosen subject to life in a way in which textbooks just cannot achieve.

It might, for example, help engage young geographers studying the decline in wild tiger populations to visit the local zoo to see the beasts up close and personal but it would be sheer folly to drop them off in the jungle covered in barbecue sauce. Similarly, sociology students tackling their crime module might spend a day in a police station to gain some insight but it would be madness to pack them off for a night in a nearby police cell. Like we said, there's a clear dividing line here.

Sadly it was one that Richard West, a physics teacher, rather stepped over in 2013 when he tried to illustrate to his class the concept of deceleration in action. Richard reasoned that making his students watch him hit the brakes of his Nissan Micra in the staff car park just wasn't going to cut it and wracked his brains for a way to demonstrate the theory.

Unwisely he hit upon the idea of firing an air gun pellet at a paper target several sheets thick and, of course, you do not need to be Sherlock Holmes to guess what happened next. The pellet scythed through the sheets of paper, rebounded off a desk and hit 17-year-old student Ben Barlow in the leg.

It was the kind of incident the school inspectors generally tend to frown upon.

An unholy row predictably ensued. Richard was suspended from his job at St Peter's Collegiate in Wolverhampton pending disciplinary proceedings, but there was a groundswell of support for the teacher amongst the student body. 'Mr West was extremely concerned and apologetic,' said Ben as he admirably tried to get his teacher off the hook. 'It was just a momentary pain, like when you walk into the corner of a table. I was left with just a scratch,' The erstwhile Secretary of State for Education, the ever-popular Michael Gove, even waded in to the debate. 'We need more whizzes and bangs in school science,' he exclaimed. 'The best science involves practicals.'

Sadly it was all to no avail and in 2014 Richard was sacked as result of his ill-judged ballistic experiment. His students were unperturbed and set up a Facebook group called 'Bring Back Westy', which garnered just shy of 3,000 Likes, three times the number of pupils actually attending St Peter's. 'Mr West has been wrongly dismissed from his position as an educator at the school,' they cried. 'This decision is disgusting and needs to be changed.'

An appeal was duly lodged against the decision and Richard was successful in getting himself reinstated. He did, however, subsequently resign his position in an apparent protest at the lack of support he felt he had received from the school in his darkest hour.

Guns, of course, have no place in the classroom, unless you happen to be enrolled at the Royal Military Academy Sandhurst, but it was not as if Richard had turned up for class dressed as Rambo brandishing an AK-47. His tale does, though, prove once again the old theory that is Murphy's Law, and that anything that can go wrong, will go wrong.

THE NORTH–SOUTH DIALECT DIVIDE

BERKSHIRE, 2013

The imminent arrival of a team of school inspectors is inevitably a stressful time for all teachers. It doesn't matter how well prepared the lesson plan or well heeled the kids, the descent of inspectors with clipboards, inscrutable expressions and the power to derail a career can be a distinctly disconcerting experience.

The number of things that can potentially go wrong while a teacher is under the critical spotlight are myriad. There's the danger of freezing under the inspectors' icy stare, the class may need reminding that Tinder is not an approved learning aid and, in extreme circumstances, the embattled educator may have to explain why the students keep asking if it's break time yet.

It was, therefore, with understandable apprehension that a secondary school in Berkshire opened its doors to the Government's educational SWAT team in 2013. Anxiety, however, turned to relief once the inspection was over and the official report concluded that it was a jolly good school indeed.

There was, though, one bizarre recommendation on their final report. One of the school's teachers happened to hail from up north – Cumbria to be precise – and the inspectors felt that it would be conducive to the children's education if she made an effort to 'sound less northern'. The school, after all, was in the Home Counties dah-ling, and certain linguistic standards had to be observed, they said in a cut-glass accent.

Inevitably there was mayhem when the unions heard about the inspectors' comments. 'She was told she needed to make her northern Cumbrian accent sound more southern,' fumed Paul Watkins of the *National Association of Schoolmasters Union of Women Teachers*. 'It was decided that would be a reasonable objective to impose upon the member. We are very disturbed by this issue and victimisation and I think this is the most extreme and bizarre objective I have ever heard of.

'It is outrageous in the extreme. You could initially see it as humorous, but the more you talk about it, the more annoyed and outraged you become. It is the most extreme form of discrimination and bullying in a country where we are supposed to be celebrating diversity. How do you assess whether her accent is more or less southern? How do you get partial success? It is the most ridiculous thing I've ever heard of.'

The good folk of Cumbria were not amused either. 'The Cumbrian accent is the most wonderful thing,' said Louise Green of the Lakeland Dialect Society. 'To try and remove it is like trying to remove Beefeaters. We should be celebrating our different regional ways of speech and promoting and protecting them.'

We can only imagine whether our unnamed Cumbrian teacher was promptly placed on a strict televisual diet of *EastEnders*, *Downton Abbey* and *Only Fools and Horses*, and forbidden from watching *Coronation Street* or her box set of *Our Friends in the North*, but it was all to no avail and there was to be no *My Fair Lady* fairy-tale ending.

The school inspectors came under intense pressure for their report and were forced into something of an embarrassing climb down. 'Negative comments about the suitability of regional accents are clearly inappropriate,' they conceded, 'and should form no part of our assessment of a school's or a teacher's performance.' More government inspectors were duly despatched to inspect the inspectors, a delicious irony which was greeted with much mirth by teachers up and down the UK.

HEADING IN THE RIGHT DIRECTION

BRISTOL, 2013

The power of the boy band over teenage girls is legendary. Scientists have shown it to be stronger than the Earth's gravitational pull, the chemical formula for superglue and the world's strongest man combined, and from the Bay City Rollers to The Jackson 5, New Kids on the Block to Take That, fresh-faced boy bands and their disturbingly suggestive dance routines have been making young ladies swoon with heart-stopping regularity.

From an educational perspective, though, boy bands are not particularly popular. It's hard enough for teachers to get some girls to focus on conjugating their French verbs or successfully solving $y = 3x^2 + x - 2$, even when they're not idly day-dreaming about becoming Mrs Justin Timberlake, while geography homework books repeatedly emblazoned with the legend 'I Love Robbie' are just irksome.

Classics teacher, Sally Knights, of Redland High School in Bristol, however, decided that if you can't beat them, you might as well join them, and cunningly decided to harness rather than harangue against the pervasive power of boy band mania.

Sally's plan was disarmingly simple. She set her 13- and 14-year-old students the task of designing a promotional poster for a band, imagining they were on tour in Ancient Greece or Rome, or write a review from a gig from the same period, and she pledged the four pupils who produced the best work would win tickets to a concert. All she had to do was secure the promised tickets, which was easier said than done. Sally was, in fact, down with the kids, and fully aware that the boy band *du jour* was One Direction, and our classics scholar went way and above the call of duty to keep her word. In fact, she spent 16 cold hours overnight on the dark streets of Cardiff queuing for the precious tickets.

'I thought it would be a bit dangerous to camp out but there were about 100 yards of 13- and 14-year-olds in tents in the queue ahead of me when I arrived,' she said. 'I was definitely one of the older ones there. I pitched my tent and had a chair. I hardly got any sleep and just read through the night.

'It was February and although it wasn't freezing, it was certainly cold. The queue started moving at 9.30a.m. the next day and it was about 10.30a.m. when I got my tickets. By the morning the queue was going around the block. The tickets for the concert sold out within a couple of minutes online but some were made available at the venue.'

According to Sally the experiment, also known as a brazen bribe, was a huge success and the scramble to win the tickets produced some stunning work. 'The artwork they produced was tremendous,' she said. 'It has helped the students understand that, like with the concert, the same things were happening with Roman gladiators – they were the superstars of their day and people would crowd to see them. Some of the girls translated some of the titles of One Direction songs into Latin. The concert is an interesting way to get the students to use Latin more and to see things in a bigger perspective.'

Sally's only regret was the temporary deafness she suffered when she announced the four lucky winners, and had to endure the high decibel screaming of a quartet of dangerously overexcited teenagers, which made the roar of the engines of a Boeing 747 sound like a gentle lullaby.

STEPHANIE'S
FACEBOOK FAUX PAS

CLEVELAND, 2014

Social media is the modern equivalent of the cartoon banana. The potential perils of an injudicious post on Facebook, Instagram *et al*, are well documented and we are all just one ill-judged key stroke away from an embarrassing slip-up online. This is why you should never, ever, under any circumstances log on when you are over-emotional, under the influence of a bottle of Rioja or taking industrial-strength medication. Auntie Mabel really doesn't need to see *those* pictures, does she?

Forward-thinking schools are forever warning students about the dangers of social media. Think before you post is the general rule, but based on the evidence of this next strange tale, educators themselves would be wise to heed their own cautionary advice.

Our unfortunate teacher is music tutor Stephanie Aird, who was evidently bored during her six-week summer break, and decided to film a series of 'comedy' videos of herself on her mobile phone and upload the results onto her Facebook page. Stephanie posted 11 bizarre clips in total and no doubt sat back and waited for the 'Likes' to flood in.

Sadly she didn't get the reaction she was hoping for. In fact she lost her job, as the parents of pupils at Dyke House Sports and Technology College in Hartlepool complained that our Steph was clearly deranged, and not someone who had any business in the classroom.

Steph's videos were certainly odd to say the least. In one she rants about her fiancé Ian taking two-and-a-half hours in the shower, while in another she discusses discovering some frozen cod sauce. In another she bemoans getting her arm stuck behind a radiator, while in one clip, for reasons presumably best know to herself, she appears with a belt wrapped around her head. Her *pièce de résistance*, however, was the video in which she rambles about the death of a pet cat.

'I come to you with an unfortunate event,' she said. 'I feel absolutely awful. Me cat got run over, not Minstrel, nah, it's Minstrel's birthday today. This other cat we haven't had for very long got run over. Ian couldn't bury it. He couldn't look at it he was so upset. So I tweeted it on Twitter and me mate Jim answered. He said "I'll come up and bury it if you like?" I said, alright then, yes please. Anyway, he's been up and buried it. Before he went out he took his shoes off – Nike Airs, £122 a pair. Only got them three days ago. While he's out there burying the cat in Ian's wellies, dog ate his Nike Air trainers. I feel like chucking the dog through the shed window like our other dog. Absolutely gutted, I feel awful. I'll have to go, bye. Oh god. Nike Air. Couldn't they have been Primark? Why can't he wear Primark trainers like every b****r else. Oh no, oh s***e.'

As soon as the head was alerted to the clips, Stephanie was suspended. The parents were not amused although she was not without supporters among the student body. 'It's an absolute joke … this girl is original, funny, witty, all with a non-offensive comedian act,' wrote one. 'She's not hurting anyone, let's support her she's a fantastic teacher and people all over Hartlepool will know she teaches pupils and inspires them.' It was too late for the 46-year-old, though, and the following month she 'quit' her job by 'mutual consent'.

Education's loss, however, was show business's gain as Stephanie announced she was going to pursue her 'comedy' and had already been booked to appear in Blackpool. 'There are certainly no hard feelings,' she said. 'I spent 18 years working there, and the school will always have a special place in my heart. But I've taken it as a kick up the backside and I'm excited about what lies ahead of me. Maybe I would have stagnated for the next ten years, so by making a break I'm determined to try and be a success.'

Stay away from Facebook, Steph, and you'll be just fine.

WHITNEY'S TELEVISED TRIBULATIONS

AUSTRALIA, 2014

In the innocent eyes of a young child, teachers can often appear omniscient. They just seem to know so much stuff and the sheer amount of knowledge they impart in the classroom five days a week can leave pupils in awe of their educators.

Sadly, though, there are times when the all-knowing veil must inevitably slip. This usually occurs when a particularly precocious pupil enquires what is the capital of Lichtenstein (it's Vaduz), or what's Queen Elizabeth's middle name (Alexandra, if you're interested). But in the embarrassing case of Australian teacher, Whitney Beseler, her dreaded moment of exposure reached a far wider audience than just her classroom.

Whitney had signed up to appear on the quiz show *Millionaire Hot Seat* on Australian TV, a spin-off from the original *Who Wants To Be A Millionaire?* She had, of course, told all her students to tune in for her appearance and was understandably chomping at the bit when her turn in the fabled chair arrived.

It was time for her first question for $100. For those of you not familiar with the format, that's the easy-peasy opener that they throw in for a bit of a giggle before contestants get down to the serious business of trying to win seven figures. Everybody gets it right. Well, almost everyone.

'Which of these is *not* a piece of jewellery commonly

worn to symbolise a relationship between two people?' asked genial Channel Nine host Eddie McGuire. 'A: Engagement ring. B: Anniversary Ring. C: Wedding Ring. D: Burger Ring.'

Not a question to trouble Mensa's finest, then. Whitney paused for thought and then suddenly suffered what she herself eloquently described as a 'brain fart' and inexplicably decided the answer was anniversary ring. The audience gasped, Eddie's face dropped and a mortified Whitney failed to win a single cent. Her pupils presumably just stared at their screens in stunned silence. 'Oh my god, Eddie,' she gasped before making her ignominious exit stage left, 'that is the most embarrassing thing that has ever happened to me before.'

To put her horror show in some context, a burger ring Down Under is a circular, corn-based savoury snack. It's the Aussie version of an onion ring and absolutely nothing whatsoever to do with jewellery, romantic or otherwise.

To add insult to injury, Whitney's desperate pleas to the show's producers to give her a face-saving second chance and let her start over were ignored and they compounded her already considerable misery by sending her home with a bag of the aforementioned Burger Rings as a consolation prize.

A STICKY SITUATION
COLOMBIA, 2014

Teachers are endlessly forced to confiscate contraband from their pupils. Rules is rules after all and should any student be foolish enough to venture into school with a prohibited item, teachers are well within their rights to impound it sharpish. There's a good reason why Game Boys and pet hamsters are a no-no in the classroom and why pupils are not allowed through the school gates brandishing baseball bats or tyre irons.

 Such confiscated items are invariably locked in a handy drawer or cupboard, stored away until the errant pupil has seen the error of their ways, but the important point here is confiscation is by definition meant to be a temporary punishment. The pupils are supposed to get their stuff back sooner or later otherwise it's just theft.

 The short-term nature of the deal, however, was rather lost on a teacher in Colombia in the summer of 2014 when he found himself competing against football fever and the impending World Cup finals for his pupils' academic attention. Specifically, our dismayed South American educator was struggling to get the kids to concentrate on their algebra and arithmetic because they had become obsessed with buying and trading Panini football stickers and in a desperate attempt to regain control of his classroom, he promptly impounded every Cristiano Ronaldo, Wayne Rooney and Lionel Messi he could lay his hands on.

'The teacher was confiscating various pupils' stickers,' reported *El Espectador* newspaper, 'arguing that a commercial market was being created that was distracting students from their academic work in the institution.'

Problem solved but the story took a surprising turn when one of the disgruntled pupils was strolling past the staff room and minding his own business when he noticed through a window his teacher hunched intently over a desk. A closer look revealed he was carefully sorting through the confiscated stickers and using them to fill the gaps in his own Panini World Cup album. He had been well and truly rumbled.

'It's no way to give an example to young ones,' complained one angry parent on the local radio station after the news of the teacher's misdemeanour emerged, 'taking their stickers away for your own benefit.'

There was, of course, uproar. The unidentified teacher was reported to the police for the heartless theft of the prized stickers while parents lodged a complaint with the local education authority. The light-fingered educator proceeded to apologise profusely for his crime but then rather ruined his act of contrition when he asked if anyone happened to have a spare Frank Lampard they were willing to swap.

ARVIND'S INDIAN MARATHON

INDIA, 2014

It is a common academic phenomenon, experienced by teachers and pupils alike, that certain lessons just seem to last longer than others. Double maths on a Friday afternoon can, for instance, frequently feel like a lifetime sentence while double sociology on Tuesday mornings seems to fly by in no time at all. Time may indeed be linear but the experience of it in the classroom is definitely all relative.

Students at the Graphic Era University in northern India could have been forgiven for thinking time had probably stopped altogether when they reported for a lecture in 2014, subjected as they were to a lesson which demanded surreal levels of scholastic stamina and no doubt sent more than a few of the poor kids a bit mental.

It was very, very long lecture indeed. In fact, it lasted for a grand total of 139 gruelling hours, 42 painfully protracted minutes and 56 agonising seconds. That's nearly six days of their young lives they'll never get back.

The madman behind the academic torture was 26-year-old Arvind Mishra, an assistant professor in mechanical engineering at the university. Arvind, of course, desperately wanted to get his name into *Guinness World Records* for the longest continuous lesson in the history of teaching and despite the protestations of his unwilling guinea pigs, proceeded to expound on the riveting topic of scientific computation for the best part of a week.

The previous record had stood at 121 hours, set by a Polish teacher by the name of Errol Muzawazi, but Arvind smashed the previous milestone and to the audible groans of the student body, continued to wibble on for 18 more hours just to prove his point.

'There's a lot I love about being a teacher,' he said after his bizarre feat. 'Teaching is one of the rarest professions that keep your brain young, allowing you to continue your own journey as a student and a lifelong learner. The one who does the teaching is the one who's doing the learning. Sharing knowledge, in my opinion, is a wonderful way of giving back what my gurus have imparted in me. The past couple of years at Graphic Era University have been such an enriching experience that I have decided to dedicate my entire life in this process of sharing and learning.'

Many of his students desperately tried to change courses after the marathon lecture was finally completed, pleading to transfer to animal husbandry or media studies, but the university was delighted with his efforts and all the free PR and handed Arvind a promotion and cheque for one lakh rupees (nearly £1,000 in sterling). His long-suffering students got nothing.

His record-breaking efforts made news around the world and the following year Arvind was invited over to France to put his levels of endurance to the test again, this time embarking on an attempt to read aloud for as long as possible. He chose *Mahabharatha*, one of the two major historical Sanskrit epics of ancient India, as his text and continuously 'entertained' his invited audience for an eye-watering 117 hours, 33 minutes and two seconds before presumably having a bit of a kip.

According to Arvind, the secret of his remarkable ability to stay awake for long periods is regular yoga. Conversely his students admitted they found his lectures the perfect cure for insomnia.

MATHEMATICS GETS SEXY
THAILAND, 2014

The publishing world has a long and colourful history of causing controversy and uproar. From Karl Marx and Friedrich Engels' *The Communist Manifesto* to Vladimir Nabokov's *Lolita*, *American Psycho* by Brett Easton Ellis to Salman Rushdie's *The Satanic Verses*, books have always had the ability to stir things up a bit.

School books, however, have tended to enjoy a gentler, less incendiary reputation. Not a single fatwa was issued, for instance, when the *Geography Revision Guide* was first published while there was a distinct lack of angry mobs on the streets when *Spelling, Punctuation and Grammar for Beginners* hit the library shelves.

One academic text, however, which did get folk rather hot under the collar was the seemingly innocent tome *Basic Mathematics,* a book published in 2014 and distributed to schools around Thailand.

It was the cover rather than the contents which caused the stink. There was no problem with either the pie or bar charts. The picture of the enthusiastic young student next to a blackboard and the image of a male teacher writing out equations were fine, too. The problem was the main picture on the book's cover – an image of an attractive, bespectacled and besuited female teacher intently reading a folder entitled 'Mathematics'.

Unfortunately for the book's publishers, she wasn't a real

teacher. She wasn't even a model posing as an educator. She was in fact Mana Aoki, one of the leading names in the Japanese adult entertainment industry. They'd printed a school book with one of Asia's top porn stars on the front of it. To compound their catastrophic error, the publishers had distributed *Basic Mathematics* without realising their mistake, sparking uproar and a hasty missive to teachers to not let their pupils anywhere near the 3,000 copies of the offending title that had already gone out. 'We will recall the problematic textbooks from every college that purchased them,' spluttered an extremely embarrassed education official. 'We will ship textbooks with new covers to them.'

The visual faux pas came out as the book's designers scoured the internet for cover images. They happened to stumble across the picture of Aoki looking suitably studious and with a quick cut and paste, they transferred the image to the front of the book. What they didn't realise what it was actually a still from one of her videos entitled 'Costume Play Working Girl' and had they watched the X-rated film, they would have seen that Aoki gets distinctly less academic and rather more amorous as the action unfolds.

The intriguing twist in the tale is who first put their hand up after the book had been distributed and admitted to recognising Aoki for who she really was? Was it one of the teachers or one of the students? Or perhaps even a parent? Unsurprisingly the identity of our whistle-blower is unrecorded.

TEA TIME IN CHINA
CHINA, 2014

Hell hath no fury like a woman scorned. This line is paraphrased from *The Mourning Bride*, penned by English playwright William Congreve in the late seventeenth century, and ever since it was committed to paper it has been oft quoted to underline a wholly misguided perception that the fairer sex tend to get a touch more cantankerous than chaps when things don't go their way.

Men, of course, can be just as wrathful as women if they feel they have been wronged and our next distasteful tale (and don't say you weren't warned) offers unpalatable evidence that fellas are frequently inclined to fits of pique.

Our naughty educator went by the name of Gao Chao, the only male teacher at a kindergarten in the city of Lianyungang in the province of Jiangsu in China. Fifty-four-year-old Gao was not a happy camper after being recently overlooked for the job as the school's new head, and he was also displeased with what he deemed a lack of due deference shown to him by his four younger female colleagues, all of whom were in their early twenties.

Gao was determined to teach his impertinent young co-workers a lesson they would not forget in a hurry. He decided – last chance now to stop reading any further – to urinate in their flasks of tea when they weren't looking. The disgusting cad.

'I first noticed there was a strange smell from my tea a

few weeks ago after I returned to the class after taking the children out to play in the playground,' said one of the teachers. 'The cups are not transparent, so it was hard to see if the liquid looked strange but there was certainly a strange smell, which also came from the thermos flasks that the tea was stored in.'

'I changed the flask and bought a new one but once I brought it to the kindergarten again I had the same problem with the strange smell. Eventually I discovered that my three colleagues had the same problem, and we thought perhaps somebody was putting something in the water.'

The teachers took their concerns to the school's boss, who advised they set up a clandestine camera in the staffroom in a bid to solve the mystery. A mobile phone with its camera pointing at their flasks was installed, hidden in a basket of soft toys, and the device duly captured Gao doing his beastly business. The police were hastily summoned and he was carted off to the station.

You would, of course, have thought that losing his job would have been the least of Gao's worries after the long arm of the law viewed the incriminating video evidence, but they apparently do things differently in China. Instead he was frogmarched to the local hospital to be tested for infectious diseases, but when the quacks gave him a clean bill of health, the police declined to charge him because he had not caused any actual bodily harm.

Even more remarkably, he didn't even get his marching orders from the school. His quartet of outraged colleagues refused to return to work until he had been dismissed, but the stand-off was eventually resolved when Gao begrudgingly agreed to pay each of them £200 in compensation for his inexcusable lavatorial antics and promised not go within five paces of their tea flasks ever again. They hastily clubbed together their cash and invested in a state-of-the-art CCTV system and a new teasmade guarded 24/7 by a particularly pugnacious Pekingese.

WHAT'S IN A NAME?
UK AND COLOMBIA, 2015

Your average teenage student is unlikely to rival the likes of Oscar Wilde or Spike Milligan with their coruscating wit but even the dullest pupil can garner a laugh should their teacher be unfortunate enough to have a silly surname. A bizarre name is the bane of an educator's life and over the years the profession has sadly lost too many Mrs Shufflebottoms and Mr Smelies, Miss Nutters and Mr Everhards, all driven from the classroom by the cruel jibes of waggish children.

In 2015 the UK press was having a slow news day – Twitter had broken and there was a dearth of cats doing anything remotely amusing – so the paper decided to ask its readers to share the silliest teachers' names they had encountered in the classroom. The results were at least funnier than watching an episode of *Last of the Summer Wine*.

Mr Jackass, Mr Hard and Mr Organ (who, of course, happened to be a biology teacher), we can assume, had very thick skins indeed or had very brief educational careers. Why Mrs Topless agreed to marry Mr Topless will forever remain a mystery while Miss Sexy presumably couldn't wait to tie to the knot to absolutely anyone. Poor old Garry Potter must have cursed J.K. Rowling each and every night after school, while Mrs Bowells the home economics teacher (obviously), and Mr Jingles had probably heard all the jokes before. Mrs Kitkat should have got a sponsorship deal from Nestlé, while it is debatable whether any pupil was daring enough to make fun to his face of the ominously titled Dr De'ath.

All humorous names without question, but the first prize for our most surreal educational title must got to a teacher in Colombia, who took the silly name game to a whole new level in 2015 when she won a two-year battle with local authorities to be officially known as Abcdefg Hijklmn Opqrst Uvwxyz.

Remarkably her alphabetically inspired rebrand saw the teacher change her name from Ladyzunga Cyborg. That, unsurprisingly, wasn't the name she was christened with but she decided it wasn't quite exotic or ridiculous enough and in 2013 she began a protracted legal battle with the Colombian National Registry to be called Abcdefg Hijklmn Opqrst Uvwxyz.

'I started looking for a name that nobody had in Colombia, or the world, so I thought Abcdefg Hijklmn Opqrst Uvwxyz,' the art and photography teacher from Bogota explained. 'I've changed my name so people wouldn't know it's me. But it's not because I was disturbed by it but because I wanted to always bring an element of surprise.'

The authorities did initially question her decision – and sanity – but Abcdefg Hijklmn Opqrst Uvwxyz was nothing if not persistent and forced through her bizarre application. 'If a civil notary had refused to modify her name in the civil registry, he would have broken his work obligations,' said a Colombian National Registry spokesman. 'Basically no matter how unusual, this is something that should always be allowed.'

When Abcdefg Hijklmn Opqrst Uvwxyz is not teaching art and photography to her presumably bemused students she admits she likes to indulge her other passion as a leather-clad dominatrix. Her alphabetical name has, however, caused some problems with her gentleman friends, who have complained her new name is no longer a practical safe word.

WHISPER IT QUIETLY
CYBERSPACE, 2015

'If you've got nothing nice to say, say nothing at all' is an admonishment frequently imparted by teachers to waspish pupils who've just reduced a classmate to tears with a jibe questioning their parentage or a dig at their dubious personal hygiene. Kids can be very cruel and teachers are constantly striving to keep their classrooms as civil as possible.

Keeping schtum is sound advice, but even the most patient teachers cannot always fight the urge to fire off a few *bons mots* of their own, and in recent years the more sharp-tongued among the profession have been taking to social media to get a few things off their chests.

In particular, they've been bombarding anonymous sharing app Whisper with their distinctly dark thoughts, as well as revelations that are enough to give any parent sleepless nights. The most disturbing examples are as follows …

'I'm a teacher and sometimes I'd like nothing more than to punch a kid right in the face and laugh.'

'Whenever I'm wrong and a student corrects me, I find a way to punish him or her without letting it be obvious.'

'I buy drugs from my former students.'

'I hate when my students tell me about their lives because I honestly don't care.'

'I'm a teacher and I hate to admit that I hate these kids sometimes … and by sometimes I mean usually.'

'I like to predict the future of my students on their looks and how they behave.'

'I'm teacher and most of the stuff I teach is useless.'

'As a teacher for the past 15 years, I make the kids watch a movie when I am hung over.'

'I'm a teacher and I mispronounce names all the time to make my students upset.'

'I'm a teacher and in my school break I smoke weed with my favourite student.'

'I used to love kids, until I trained as a teacher, now I can't stand them.'

'I'm a teacher. My ten years make me concerned for the future.'

'Sometimes I can't believe how stupid some of my pupils are.'

'As a teacher I find it hard to be nice to the popular girls because I hated them when I was at school.'

'I'm not supposed to have favourite students, but I definitely do.'

'During the day I'm a teacher, by night I'm a stripper

because let's face it, teaching itself doesn't pay the bills.'

'I'm a teacher and I had sex with another teacher in the classroom.'

'I'm a teacher and when the kids go outside for recess, I watch porn.'

'How can I ask 30 teenagers to respect me when I don't even respect myself?'

As an advert for the profession, it is not a catalogue of quotes to instil incredible confidence, but it does prove teachers are nothing if not human. In the interests of balance, it's also true there were one or two uplifting Whisper posts and while they were still very much in the minority, they proved not every educator is a subversive, student-hating malcontent. 'The biggest way I could let my students down is if they don't see how much I care about them,' wrote one. 'I worry more about that than anything else.'

Should Whisper ever suffer a catastrophic data leak and hackers reveal the identities of the teachers in question, they'll have a lot more than that to worry about.

A PRESENT
FROM THE PAST
MISSOURI, USA, 2015

The end-of-year ritual that sees appreciative pupils giving their teachers presents is not one likely to eclipse Christmas in the luxury gift stakes anytime soon. There's only so much talcum powder, soap and cheap toiletries any educator needs, a homemade card is cute but it's going straight in the bin and the excitement at the rare appearance of a bottle of wine quickly disappears after the first exploratory sip and the gagging subsides.

No, teachers stoically accept that the end of term merely means an exponential increase in the amount of useless tat they possess and they really should be up for an Oscar for their ability to plaster on a grateful smile after receiving another box of supermarket sweets because the parents couldn't even stretch to a box of Begian chocolates.

There are, of course, exceptions to every rule, and in 2015 a home economics teacher from Missouri called Marilyn Mecham, was presented with a gift that really was worth receiving. Lucky Marilyn got a cheque for $10,000 from a former student she had taught almost four decades earlier.

Our beneficent ex-pupil went by the name of Kevin Perz, a 56-year-old from Kansas City who'd done rather well for himself in the construction business after graduating from Parkway Central High School back in 1977, and decided it was high time to repay the efforts of the teachers who had set him on his path to considerable success.

Our Kev had already successfully tracked down his maths teacher in 1992 to express his gratitude with a $5,000 gift, and a decade later touched base with his former business tutor to hand over a cheque for $10,000, but locating the elusive Marilyn at first proved more tricky until officials at Parkway finally found an address for her son. Kev got on the phone and within days a handwritten letter and 10,000 big ones were on their way to Marilyn.

'I sent the first note to my senior year calculus teacher, Mr Putz,' Kevin told Today.com. 'I never worked hard until Mr Putz's class. He's the reason I was able to eventually get an engineering degree. So, when I had the means to do so, I sent him $5,000 and a thank-you note. That was over 20 years ago now.'

'Someone from the alumni association went through these 40-year-old pay records, and, at long last, she found Mrs Mecham. She was the best. She set it up so that we were always able to get our work done, but still have a ton of fun. She really connected with the kids. I never forgot her smile.'

The gift came with the strict instructions that Marilyn should spend the money on herself, which prompted an even broader smile than usual. 'I was so appreciative to have somebody spend all that time looking for you to tell that you meant so much in their life,' she said. 'Gratitude is something in this society today that we just don't do enough of.

'I got this big envelope from the mailbox and I just thought, "How cool is this?" I was already tearing up just reading the letter. It really took me back. And then I noticed that he'd written something about a gift. I looked and there was this check face down, and I turned it over and saw the word 'thousand'. What? I was overwhelmed. I just stood there in silence. It was humbling and surreal.'

Kev's altruistic actions certainly captured the public imagination but he did come to rather regret his generosity when his phone suddenly went into meltdown as every single one of his erstwhile teachers suddenly called to enquire how the hell he was.

CARTEL BOSS IN THE CLASSROOM

MEXICO, 2015

Drugs sadly are a growing problem in our schools and modern educators need to be ever vigilant for the telltale signs of the use of illicit narcotics. Pupils, for example, who seem to require an inordinate amount of silver foil to wrap their sandwiches should be watched like hawks while certain students are probably best not left unsupervised with a Bunsen burner.

Regrettably some teachers have also been known to chase the dragon or powder their nose (which we are reliably led to believe both mean – on da' street – to take drugs) but the general rule is the vast majority of educators are on the front line in the war *against* illegal substances rather than fully signed-up members of the Robert Downey Jr. or Keith Richards fan clubs. The bad apples who do let the academic side down usually fall foul of a 'funny cigarette' at a party (or so they claim), but an altogether more wholesale example of a teacher dabbling in drugs can be found in Mexico, with the startling tale of Servando Gómez Martínez.

To his primary school pupils in the town of Arteaga in the state of Michoacan, he seemed like any other teacher, but in reality Martínez was a founder member of La Familia, one of Mexico's leading and ultra-violent drug cartels. He went on to to become the feared boss of the infamous Knights Templar cartel and he made billions of pesos flooding the United States with methamphetamine and cocaine.

Martínez was at the height of his criminal powers in the 2000s but remarkably he remained listed on the payroll at the school in Arteaga until 2009, his scholastic background earning him the nicknames in narcotic circles of 'La Tuta' ('The Teacher') and 'El Profe' ('The Professor'). If his students knew what was good for them, they simply called him 'Sir' and made absolutely sure they never failed to hand in their homework in on time.

Martínez's bloody reign of terror finally came to an end in 2015, when security services armed to the teeth finally caught up with him after trailing his girlfriend as she delivered a chocolate cake, and he was promptly banged up in Mexico City to await what promises to be a hefty custodial sentence. Since his arrest his former pupils have wisely kept their counsel on whether 'La Tuta' was a good teacher or not but one did admit on the condition of absolute anonymity that he had a particular fondness for chemistry lessons.

SISTER
CAUGHT IN THE ACT
PHILADELPHIA, USA, 2015

'To Alcohol! The cause of – and solution to – all of life's problems.' The immortal words of Homer Simpson – and what tired teacher has not at times reached for the demon drink at the end of a gruelling day in an attempt to expunge some of the more stressful memories of six-and-a-half hours in the chaos that is the classroom? Every educator needs a tipple from time to time.

Sister Kimberley Miller was evidently feeling particularly parched after her shift at the Little Flower Catholic High School for Girls in Philadelphia in 2015. Even nuns like a drink, you know, and what with it being a Friday night, Sister Kimberley decided to remove her wimple and let her hair down a bit.

Unfortunately she then got into her car well past the midnight hour and drove off. She ended up in a parking lot and smashed into the glass entrance door of a shop, a collision which inevitably attracted the attention of the police who pulled her over and asked our libatious bride of Christ to take a sobriety test. She failed.

To compound Kim's misfortune, the whole sorry incident was captured on the dashboard camera of a passing motorist, and it was not long before her well-lubricated but doomed attempts to walk in a straight line and stand steady on one foot to convince the cops she hadn't touched a drop, honestly officer, were amusing YouTube viewers worldwide.

It was certainly not behaviour befitting a nun, and when the owner of the shop she had almost demolished arrived at work the next day, the story had become big news. 'Randomly that someone hits your building, and then to find out it was a nun who happened to be drunk at almost three in the morning on a Friday night, it's not something you expect to walk into on a Saturday morning,' the owner told reporters. 'The officer explained to me, he said, "Someone hit your building. It was a nun who happened to be drunk and we arrested her".'

The Sister was promptly placed on suspension after her inebriated antics but God must have been looking out for her as her pupils hastily organised a petition in her support and after gathering an impressive 1,800 signatures, fired it off to the Archdiocese of Philadelphia's Office of Catholic Education.

'Sister Kim has served the Little Flower community and its students for many years,' it read. 'She has helped her students blossom into the women they are today with her selfless devotion and dedication to her faith and job as a teacher. She has been a fine educator and a shoulder to cry on for many of her students. Her wisdom and love has helped many of her students get through the most difficult times of high school. In light of recent events, all of the positive things she has done should not be overshadowed by one negative wrongdoing. If Sister Kim has had a significant effect on you during your years at Little Flower, help to reinstate her job by signing this petition.'

The burning question of course is how Kimberley managed to get quite so slaughtered. Some speculated she had been at the communion wine while others insisted she had partaken in one bottle too many of Blue Nun.

THE ERRANT
ELECTRICAL ARTIST

OREGON, USA, 2015

Marking is one of the monotonous realities of the teaching profession. As inevitably as night follows day, setting homework entails teachers deploying their faithful red biros to assess the results and many a mental breakdown among educators has been attributed to the daunting sight of a pile of 30 maths books sitting there, screaming out to be marked. Like painting the Forth Bridge, it's an endless task and the only release comes with the summer holidays, early retirement or, in extreme circumstances, pleading temporary insanity.

It was, however, marking of a shockingly different nature that caused American teacher Samuel Dufner problems in 2015 as he taught science to a class of teenage pupils at South Salem High School in Oregon. Silly Samuel took his marking rather too far and ended up being arrested by the boys in blue.

Samuel was trying to demonstrate the chemical reactions caused by electrical charges. To do so, he dusted off his trusty Telsa coil, a type of wireless electrical transformer, for the job and asked his class for volunteers. There was no shortage of willing guinea pigs and Samuel proceeded to illustrate the power of electricity by giving the volunteers a brief shock from the Telsa coil, which left temporary burn marks on their skin.

Point proven. But Samuel unwisely allowed his artistic

side get the better of him and proceeded to give pupils 'I ♥ Mom' tattoos to really ram home his scientific message. To be fair, the marks were merely temporary and did fade, but not before the kids had gone home for the day and many parents predictably took a dim view of his methods and beat an angry path to the principal's door. Possibly carrying pitch forks and burning torches.

'He took like the probe and he touched my hand and I pulled my hand away and it was done,' said one student in his defence. 'It hurt me a little bit, but as soon as I pulled my hand away the pain was gone.' Another of the teenagers added: 'He was making, like, smiley faces and stars, but some students wanted to see how long they could hold it there. Almost every student did it, and everyone was laughing when they went up there.'

The pupils' support fell on deaf ears, however, and Samuel was promptly arrested on suspicion of criminal mistreatment, a police investigation ensued and he was suspended pending further enquiries. 'By law he has a duty to protect them,' said Lieutenant Steve Birr. 'He inflicted the burns and, in fact, assaulted them.'

Things looked bleak for Samuel but it subsequently emerged he had been conducting the same, tattoo-themed scientific experiment at the school for years without complaint or censure and common sense eventually prevailed. The District Attorney's office deemed there was no crime to answer for and decided Samuel would not be 'charged'. Which is, of course, more than could be said of his students.

POST MORTEM FELINE FROLICS

OKLAHOMA, USA, 2015

It is one of education's oldest adages that the behaviour of a class reflects directly on the teacher who has been tasked with turning them into reasonably respectable members of society. A class that minds its Ps and Qs, helps old ladies cross the road and has never seen the inside of a police cell makes a teacher look at least competent, while a mob of students whose antics makes the invasion of the Viking hordes look like innocent tomfoolery are the stuff of an educator's nightmares.

Consequently, it was much to the chagrin of an anonymous science teacher at the Harding Charter Preparatory High School in Oklahoma, that her pupils became something an Internet sensation. You may have already deduced their online notoriety came about for all the wrong reasons.

Picture the macabre scene: a group of students dressed in white lab coats lined up in front of the camera; each student is holding a dead cat, destined for dissection in their biology class. Someone hits play on iTunes, and to the musical accompaniment of the jingle of a well-known cat food commercial, the youngsters proceed to choreograph their feline cadavers in a dance extravaganza. Think Michael Jackson's 'Thriller' with deceased moggies.

As you might have already anticipated, the resulting video found its way onto Facebook and then YouTube and all hell broke loose. 'I think it's really a stain on their reputation and they need to do something to stop this and make sure it doesn't happen again,' said a spokeswoman for the Oklahoma branch of the Humane Society of the United States. 'If you think of a beloved family pet that you care about that's ended up being euthanized, then sold to a dealer, and this is how their body is treated, I don't think anybody would approve of that.'

The exact whereabouts of our unnamed biology teacher while her students were disgracing themselves is unclear, but a grovelling apology to her boss behind closed doors was seemingly enough to avoid the sack. 'Most of the students in the video were no longer students here when I had received the video, so they were not punished,' said the principal. 'I have had conversations with the teacher. She has ensured me that this will never happen again. This is completely out of character for our students and especially our staff. The perception that this video creates is not one that we would like to be out there. In my opinion, we have handled this situation in the hopes that it will never happen again.'

Quite. All animal corpses at Harding Charter scheduled for dissection are now kept safely under lock and key, and only released to students once rigor mortis has set in, the logic presumably being that it's bloody hard to get a dead cat to do John Travolta in *Saturday Night Fever* when it's as stiff as a board.

CLASSROOM CONFESSIONS
CYBERSPACE, 2015

A problem shared is allegedly a problem halved. King Solomon famously almost took the adage too literally when he threatened to chop a young lad in two in a bid to resolve a maternity dispute between two women, but the salient point here is that talking over your problems and darkest secrets can be cathartic.

Educators are no different and when the 'We are Teachers' website invited members of the profession to divulge their most embarrassing and shameful classroom misdemeanours, which they had hitherto not dared share with colleagues, family or friends, they were deluged with bizarre tales of educational misadventure.

The flood of colourful (albeit anonymous) confessions kicked off with the teacher who was inadvertently responsible for depriving a pupil of their underwear. 'One of the boys in my class had an accident. I had seen my mother clean underwear out by holding it in the toilet and flushing. Well, I never thought about how much more pressure toilets in a school would have. As I flushed, the underwear flew down the pipe.'

Unfortunate bodily functions featured again when a pregnant educator found the subtle aromas wafting from the school kitchen rather overwhelming. 'While teaching a lesson, I caught a whiff of the cafeteria food and instantly felt queasy. I couldn't make it to the bin, so I threw up in my cupped hands in front of the class. I didn't know what to do and I couldn't leave them to go wash up, so I shook my hands off, sent a student to get some wet paper towels from the bathroom and kept teaching.'

The myriad dangers of the World Wide Web were underlined by the educator who turned to a well-known search engine for help with a spot of translation: 'In a German lesson on fruit, I googled melons and got more than I bargained for.'

Accidental slips of the tongue were well represented with many teachers wishing they had heeded the old advice that it's prudent to think before you speak. 'I have one of those plastic pointers that look like a hand with the finger as the pointer. I handed it to a student and said, "Bill, would you please give Jenny the finger?"'

Another linguistic slip saw an exam invigilator drop a comical clanger. 'I had tutored students taking a progress test. One student was gazing at the computer screen for a very long time. I asked if something was wrong and he replied, "I am thinking." I replied, "Stop thinking and finish the test." The other two teachers in the room promptly doubled over with laughter.'

Rudimentary guitar lessons meanwhile saw another teacher end up with egg all over their face. 'I gave all the six-year-olds rulers, and everyone held them in front to "strum". I said to the one student who didn't do this, "That's not the way to hold a guitar". One of the other kids said, "He only has one arm!"'

Amnesia, however, rather than foot-in-mouth disease was the cause of the pick of the confessional bunch. 'My history class was taking a test. All was quiet until I heard a commotion. On the matching section of the test, I had failed to remove the answers before making copies.'

God help the teaching profession and its numbers should the educational Stasi ever choose to trace the IP addresses of those who contributed to the 'We are Teachers' online conversation and pop round after dark for a 'quiet word'.

ARNIE'S DELAYED ARRIVAL

NEW JERSEY, USA, 2015

It was Louis XVII, the French monarch in the early nineteenth century, who observed that 'punctuality is the politeness of kings'. Judging by his exceedingly portly depiction in contemporary portraits, not-so-little Louis was never late for his lunch but his point about the importance of turning up on time still holds water. As evidently did Louis based on his aforementioned rotundity.

Tardiness in students is a well-documented phenomenon but teachers, of course, are supposed to set a good example to the kids when it comes to time-keeping, which makes the erratic behaviour of American educator Arnold Anderson all the harder to justify.

Arnie, as we shall henceforth call him, was not exactly the embodiment of punctuality. In fact, in the two academic years ending in the summer of 2015 he was late for work at Roosevelt Elementary School in New Brunswick in New Jersey a staggering 111 times.

The frustrated principal privately lamented that he couldn't put Arnie in detention and the school was forced to take more drastic action to address his repeated inability to show his face before the school bell rang and tried to sack him. Arnie summoned the union reps and called in the lawyers and the dispute went to arbitration.

Remarkably he dodged the bullet. The arbitrator conceded he should invest in a new alarm clock as a matter of urgency but ruled that he was entitled to progressive discipline and that the school had neither issued him with any written warnings nor given him 90 days grace in which to sort himself out. The arbitrator did, however, reject Arnie's bold assertion that the quality of his teaching outweighed the crime of being regularly late.

His case was resolved (if not to the satisfaction of the school) but that did not stop the story becoming something of a political hot potato when Republican Governor Chris Christie (no, we're not making that up) waded angrily into the debate. 'Think I'm too tough on the teachers' union?' he fumed. 'This is what we're dealing with in New Jersey.'

We have not, however, yet reached the best bit of our story and that, of course, is the reason for Arnie's tardiness. It was not heavy traffic on the freeway (as the Americans will insist on calling their roads) and it was not due to over-running engineering works on the railways. He didn't even claim the dog had eaten the kids' homework. No, Arnie was late 111 times because he got peckish when he woke up. 'I have a bad habit of eating breakfast in the morning and I lost track of time,' he admitted. 'I have now cut out eating breakfast at home. I will be early.'

To be fair, Arnie was true to his word and eliminated his late shows but his first class of the school day was rather regularly disrupted as he polished off a plate of pancakes at his desk.

THE ELUSIVE SPROUT SMUGGLER

CAMBRIDGESHIRE, 2015

Little scamps that they are, children are forever bringing things into school with them. Sadly it is not always their homework, their sports kit or an unquenchable thirst for knowledge, and teachers frequently find themselves cast in the role of prison guards as they strive to intercept contraband. It's frightening how adeptly a cunning seven-year-old can conceal an elicit packet of Haribo Starmix, while there are kids who will relentlessly attempt to surreptitiously get their Pokémon cards into the classroom despite the threat of spending a day in the sweatbox.

It was prohibited items of an altogether more bizarre nature, however, which plagued Monkfield Park Primary School in Cambridgeshire in 2015, as bemused staff struggled to capture one of the most fiendish juvenile smugglers in living memory. It was a battle of wits that made Kasparov versus Fischer look like a dunce's convention.

The contraband in question was Brussels sprouts. Cooked Brussels sprouts to be accurate, which a child was seemingly bringing into school and then secretly depositing into the bags of other, unsuspecting kids. We can only presume they had been proffered at home at mealtimes, and rather than risk the wrath of their parents by not eating their seasonal delicacies, our smuggler had stashed them away and 'redistributed' them among the rest of the school. It was December and nearly Christmas after all.

The spotlight of suspicion fell on one class, but despite extensive investigations that would have put Hercule Poirot to shame, the culprit could not be identified. 'These Brussels sprouts have been discovered in children's bags, we think in an effort to dispose of them,' wrote headmistress Sarah Jarman in a plea to parents to help unmask the phantom vegetable runner. 'Since we have children in school with severe food allergies, this is obviously a situation which we require your assistance in monitoring.'

Exactly how many people are actually allergic to Brussels sprouts, rather than just hating the taste, is a moot point, but the search for the sprout smuggler continued, and as the days went by, the master criminal of Monkfield Park garnered quite the fan club. 'When I read the letter I laughed,' one parent told reporters who had nothing better to do. 'I thought it was a wind-up. The kid should get a medal and a job with MI5. They're a genius. The kid hid the sprouts from his mum and dad, probably got praise for eating them, then sneaked them into school.'

In a blow for the ingenuity of the younger generation, the Brussels brigand was never apprehended, although the flow of green spherical vegetables into school did eventually come to an end.

An interesting footnote to our tale is the date on which it hit the local and national newspapers. The story was widely reported on 3 December, which any student could tell you is 22 full days before Christmas, rather begging the question of what kind of twisted parents were feeding their poor kid sprouts three weeks before the big day. That takes child cruelty to a whole new level.

SPELLING IT OUT
KENT, 2016

The frequently fractious debate as to whether spelling is still relevant in the modern world has been waged for some time. The traditionalists argue it matters lest we confuse 'there' and 'their' and open up a Pandora's Box of linguistic chaos, while the texting generation are adamant 'ur' is equally as serviceable as 'your', and '2mrw' a perfectly good substitute for 'tomorrow'.

Teachers of ten- and 11-year-old students, however, know that spelling matters. Especially if their charges are to prosper in their end-of-year SATS tests, not bring shame on the school and, most importantly of all, not see the aforementioned educators summoned to the head's office to receive an angry ticking off.

When SATS do rear their ugly heads, frantic teachers try to ensure their pupils are up to speed, but in this chastening tale of being hoisted by your own petard, it is worth remembering that educators should practise what they preach.

Our unfortunate, unnamed teacher hails from Kent. He (for we do know he's a chap) was evidently concerned about the spelling proficiency of one of his pupils and decided to send a cautionary note home with the young lad. It read:

For homework each week, I will be sending home six words from the recommended spelling test which I will then pick up in class the following work [sic]. Please try to help you [sic] child learn these as it will make a huge difference.

Week 1
Accommodate
Communicate
Equip
Immediateley [sic]
Physical
Sincerley [sic]

Oh dear, oh dear: four spelling mistakes in a letter about the importance of spelling. He was, of course, far from the first teacher to suffer a typing malfunction and his error may have gone unadmonished had it not been for the fact the boy's mother was a big fan of Twitter and immediately took to the social media platform to share his discomfort with her followers. 'My son has spellings from school that they want him to learn,' she wrote under the handle Pandamoanimum, 'I'm currently holding my head and sighing.'

Twitter went wild. Not as wild as the time Kim Kardashian posted a picture of herself actually wearing clothes, but febrile nonetheless, and mummy's original post was soon retweeted almost 2,000 times. 'There's no excuse anymore surely,' wrote one outraged follower, 'what with spellcheck etc.' while another saw the funny side and wryly urged her to 'communicate them immediateley and accomadate a meeting to physically equip them with the facts. Sincereley.' The wag.

There were, however, cynics who suggested that Pandamoanimum had used Photoshop to change the letter in an attempt to shame the teacher for reasons unknown but she was unrepentant. 'This is unfortunately totally genuine,' she wrote. 'It was stuck into my ten-year-old son's literacy homework book. If you think it's fake, then that's your prerogative. But it's not. I don't care if you think it's fake. I haven't shamed anyone as I have mentioned no names, the teacher or the school and, obviously, wouldn't name them on social media either. I will, of course, be going into the school and questioning why something so littered with errors was sent home. I appreciate and value teachers, but errors like that are just not on.'

The outcome of the meeting remained private and the last word on the whole sorry business must go to another Tweeter who rather got to the heart of the matter. 'Speaking as a teacher,' they wrote, 'it was probably written at 2a.m. after marking 90 books and drinking the best part of a bottle of red.' Teachers turning to the demon drink in times of stress and a heavy workload? Perish the thought.

JUDITH'S PARENTAL JIBE
SOMERSET, 2016

The role of the headteacher is a multifaceted one, which demands a myriad talents dealing, as the school's *grand fromage* must, with such diverse groups as local authority politicians, pupils, fellow educators, parents and the chap who wants a cheque for repainting the science lab after that unfortunate episode involving a can of hairspray and a faulty light switch.

The head must be seen to be unequivocally in charge and yet his or her door must always be open to those within the school community so that dialogue can be maintained. A successful head, in short, must be able to dangle the carrot but not be afraid to wield the stick.

It's a tricky balancing act, and one which headmistress Judith Barrett of St Michael's Academy in Yeovil somewhat misjudged in 2016, when she became increasingly frustrated with the disturbingly dishevelled appearance of pupils turning up for school. Standards had to be upheld, Judith reasoned, but her letter to parents was nothing if not direct.

'Unfortunately I have noticed an increasing number of children who are coming to school in a pretty shocking state,' she wrote. 'They are dirty, unkempt and not in appropriate school uniform, if in any uniform at all. Today, being that it is a Monday, quite a few have returned to school in dirty clothes and obviously haven't had a shower in readiness for

Monday morning. There are also an increasing number who are not making any attempt to wear black school shoes, in line with school policy.

'There are also a lot of children who are getting themselves up in the morning and into school as their parents are still in bed. In a country where there is plentiful running water and washing machines, and shops like Tesco offering entire school uniforms for £10, it is a pretty poor indictment of the parenting skills of some of our families.

'I totally appreciate that life is hard for some of you but please make sure that your children are clean and ready for school and that includes the correct clothes. Starting next week I intend phoning home to contact parents of children not in uniform, including black shoes, and you will be asked to take them home.'

Blimey. It is, of course, page one in the headteacher's big book of best practice not to go around casting aspersions on the 'parenting skills' of the mums and dads. They just don't like it and the parental backlash was as swift as it was predictable. 'It will make the child feel like utter poo,' raged one, 'but the other children will have a good laugh at said child where a parent can't be bothered.'

In her defence, Judith claimed she was merely trying to raise the school's most recent rating from good to outstanding. 'The school is well led and managed at all levels,' read that report, 'with governors successfully supporting the principal's outstanding vision and decisive leadership.' 'Decisive' in that particular context presumably meaning 'sledgehammer'.

OTHER TITLES IN

THE
STRANGEST®
SERIES

The *Strangest* series has been delighting and enthralling readers for decades with weird, exotic, spooky and baffling tales of the absurd, ridiculous and the bizarre. This range of fascinating books – from Football to London, Rugby to Law and many subjects in between – details the very curious history of each one's funniest, oddest and most compelling characters, locations and events.

9781910232910

9781910232866

GOLF'S STRANGEST ROUNDS

9781910232934

KENT'S STRANGEST TALES

9781910232972

LAW'S STRANGEST CASES

9781910232897

LONDON'S STRANGEST TALES

9781910232880

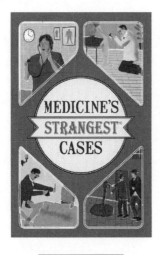

9781910232941

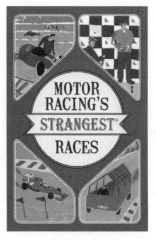

9781910232965

9781910232873

9781910232927

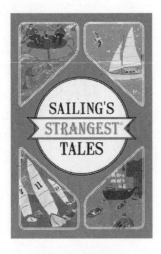

SAILING'S STRANGEST TALES

9781911042259

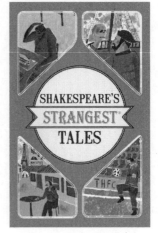

SHAKESPEARE'S STRANGEST TALES

9781910232903

256

TENNIS'S STRANGEST MATCHES

9781910232958